What others are saying about this book:

"Joan Gustafson's book is a needed and insightful approach to perceiving life's possibilities. I recommend it to parents, educators and business executives for themselves as well as to reinforce the reality that some of us, but not all of us, know 'a woman can do that!'"
—Laraine Rodgers, vice president, Emerald Solutions.

"Joan Gustafson has written the perfect book for any woman wishing to achieve success. In *A Woman Can Do That!*, she gives ten strategies that can change a woman's life, along with the proof on how they have worked for herself and others."
—Marilyn Meredith, Writers Digest instructor and author, *Deadly Omen*, the Deputy Tempe Crabtree Mystery Series.

"Terrific book! Joan Gustafson has provided an excellent road map for a successful life, as well as a successful career. She provides strategies which have been tried and proven to work by numerous women. A must-read for all women interested in improving their lives and making a contribution to the world around them."
—Bobbie Stevens, Ph.D., president, Unlimited Futures, LLC, author, *Unlimited Futures: How to Understand the Life You Have and Create the Life You Want.*

"Inspirational and uplifting! A book every woman should read! Joan Gustafson is a great example to all of us. Thank you, Joan, for writing this book for us!"
—Dee Ray, senior vice president, John G. Kinnard & Company; author, *Women, Money, and Emotions.*

"*A Woman Can Do That!* is a wonderfully practical guide to helping you achieve your goals and dreams. Create your vision, practice the strategies, build your confidence and you will be rewarded with a life that you can look back on with pride, joy and satisfaction."
—Constance B. Wolf, president, CBW, Inc.

"Joan Gustafson has an exceptional ability to bring others to the same level of dedication and passion she has for the task at hand. She coaches and builds confidence in others to reach higher than they've ever reached before. Many careers and lives have blossomed under her tutelage. She is a living example of what she teaches in her book."
  —Joan C. McBride, retired, 3M Public Relations and Corporate
    Communications Department.

"Congratulations to Joan Gustafson on a wonderful book! She has overcome a lot and accomplished a lot in her life. She is an inspiration!"
  —Cynthia Metcalf, human factors analyst, Salt Lake City, Utah.

"The strategies found in *A Woman Can Do That!* are powerful tools for any woman to use in setting and reaching her goals."
  — Linda M. Herold, founder, Women of Scottsdale; publisher, "The
    Herold Report."

"I just finished reading *A Woman Can Do That!*, and I loved it! It explains some basic laws of nature, which will help women and men take charge of their lives and experience the results in overall success. There should, for sure, be a sequel—*A Man Can Do That!*"
  —Dean M. Portinga, Th.D., Ph.D.; executive vice president, Un-
    limited Futures, LLC; Author, *Spiritual Insights.*

"I've learned so much from Joan Gustafson regarding individual career development. Her positive influence on so many people, both women and men, will be with them well into the future."
  —Steve Schumacher, International e-Business manager, 3M.

"It is often difficult to juggle all the things a woman needs in to do in order to be successful. *A Woman Can Do That!* is an inspiring and easy-reading book that gives practical tools that enable any woman to succeed in what appears to be a man's world."
  —Charleen Tajiri, founder and CEO, VisionHealth.

"When I met Joan, it was towards the end of her successful and long tenure with a Fortune 500 company. A number of the women there confided in me that Joan had been instrumental in their career development. Based on their results, Joan's own experiences and those of the other women in the book, the information she's provided should assist anyone in achieving all the success they can dream of—anyone who believes they can do it!"
  —Terry Swack, vice president, Experience Design, Razorfish.

A Woman
Can Do That!

A Woman
Can Do That!

*10 Strategies
for Creating Success in Your Life*

Joan Eleanor Gustafson

*Best wishes
for success!
Joan Gustafson*

Leader Dynamics

Manufactured in the United States of America

LCCN: 00-135398

ISBN: 0-9703026-0-6

Production by Tabby House

Cover by John Murdock Design

Front cover photo by Linda Enger Photography

**Publisher's Cataloging-in-Publication
(Provided by Quality Books, Inc.)**

Gustafson, Joan Eleanor
     A woman can do that! : 10 strategies for creating
success in your life / Joan Eleanor Gustafson. -- 1st
ed.
     p. cm.
     Includes bibliographical references (p.) and index
     LCCN 00-135398
     ISBN 0-9703026-0-6

     1. Women--Life skills guides. 2. Success in
business. 3. Self-realization. I. Title.

HF5386.G87 2001   650.1'082
                  QBI00-901634

Leader Dynamics
P.O. Box 19507
Fountain Hills, AZ 85269
publisher@leaderdynamics.com

Dedication

To my mother, Betty Notto,
who taught me the true meaning of success through her example,
and
to my husband, Cliff Gustafson,
who contributes every day to my success through his support
and encouragement

Acknowledgments

Throughout my life, I have witnessed the synergistic power of teamwork. In writing this book, I have come to realize more than ever how the combination of the talents and efforts of multiple individuals can produce a better outcome. I am grateful to all of those who have been an inspiration to me and those who have contributed to fulfilling my vision of a book that will help women create success in their lives.

I interviewed eighteen successful women, who unselfishly shared their lives and insights with me so that others may benefit. Although I did not know most of these women before the interviews, I now consider them my friends and appreciate their individual and collective contributions. A special thanks to each of them: Nancy Albertini, Lois Crandell, Gayle Crowell, Dr. Jeanne Elnadry, Linda Herold, Beth MacDonald, Mollie Young Marinovich, Betty Notto, Dee Ray, Wendy Franz Richards, Laraine Rodgers, Joan T. Smith, Dr. Bobbie Stevens, Terry Swack, Charleen Tajiri, Dr. Kathy Brittain White, Laurie Windham, and Constance B. Wolf. To this list of successful women, I add my appreciation to Sara Arbel and Connie Carroll for also sharing their stories with me.

From Dr. Dean Portinga and Dr. Dennis Deaton, I learned some consummate truths that helped me to accelerate the pace on my personal road to success. I am grateful to these two men for the knowledge they share and the work they are doing.

Many thanks to my friends and colleagues who gave of their time by transcribing interviews and proofreading early versions of the manuscript: Gloria Aguirre, Vickie Beaulieu, Shelley Berube, Cathy Charleston, Lisa Hartl, Carolyn Jensen, Cynthia Metcalf, and Carla Teetzel. Each of them helped in her own way to enhance the book.

It is with deep appreciation that I also acknowledge my editor Leni Reiss for her care and patience in editing my original manuscript.

Finally, I am grateful to each woman who has touched my life. By doing so, she has contributed not only to my success, but also to the successes of the readers of this book.

Contents

Introduction

A Woman Can Do That!

When I was in the ninth grade, I had the opportunity to spend a day with my uncle Ralph at the office building where he worked. He was a computer programmer during the era of first-generation computers, when a computer filled a room the size of a gymnasium and had a minute fraction of the power of a current notebook computer. However, even without knowing that computer power would take giant leaps forward as technology accelerated over the next several years, I was impressed and intrigued with this fascinating machine.

Uncle Ralph demonstrated the control center for the computer, which was a console typewriter device in the middle of the room. To enhance his demonstration, he instructed me to type my name on this console. He had previously programmed the computer to give me some information about my family and myself when it recognized my first name. I was amazed that the computer knew so much about me, and I understood that Uncle Ralph had been the one to teach the computer what it knew.

On the drive home, I told my uncle that I had decided that day that I also wanted to be a computer programmer. After hearing of my decision, he hesitated for a moment before speaking. He then looked at me and said, "I suppose a woman could do that, but, of course, she would never be paid as much as a man."

This happened in the early 1960s. At that time, my thoughts were the same as Uncle Ralph's. I felt that it would be a privilege to get into this field, and I would not expect my pay to ever equal that of a man. As young as I was, I was old enough to comprehend that I was living in a man's world, and I was grateful that I might have the opportunity to do the things I wanted to do in this male-oriented world.

Now that we are living in the twenty-first century, things have changed. At least, they have changed for me. Although I have taken many detours along the way, I have achieved success in what I previously had believed to be a man's world.

I recently retired from a high-ranking management position in a large, multinational corporation. If success would be measured in financial income and material possessions alone, I would rank among the most successful American women of my generation. Even though I am a woman, my annual income has been in the top one percent of that of all Americans throughout most of my career. I have lived and worked in Europe, as well as in the United States, and have received numerous awards for leadership. Over the past several years, I have owned two or three houses simultaneously in various parts of the United States, and my husband and I have traveled extensively around the world. In addition, I am blessed with more important, nonmaterial gifts of life—a loving husband, wonderful children, and beautiful grandchildren.

Although many people believe that success is predetermined and that successful people are born, not made, this was not true for me. My beginnings in life were humble. My parents were married while they still were in high school, and I was born the next year. My brother Lenny entered the world a year later while my parents were still teenagers, and our family later grew to include three more brothers and a sister. My mother stayed at home with the children while my dad worked long, hard hours repairing automobiles in order to make sure there was food on the table.

Almost single-handedly, my dad built us a house in a rural suburb of St. Paul, Minnesota, when I was four years old. The house had four rooms—a kitchen, a living room, and two bedrooms. It had no bathroom and no running water the first year we lived there. We had an outhouse as well as an outside pump. Each day, my mother pumped water for drinking and heated it on the stove for cooking and bathing. In Minnesota, the temperature was well below zero on many winter days while my mother was outdoors pumping water.

I was a shy child, and I carried this shyness into adulthood. I also had low self-esteem, an extraordinarily high fear of rejection, and a strong desire to please other people. It was probably because of this that I accepted a marriage proposal for the wrong reasons. I was engaged at age eighteen, married at age nineteen, and became a mother a year later.

I was a perfectionist and worked hard to succeed. I excelled at my full-time job and at the university courses I took at night. Between work and school, I helped the children with their homework, maintained a relatively spotless house, cooked well-balanced meals, and even ironed my husband's underwear. As a result of my attempting to be a superwoman, both my marriage and my health deteriorated. As an adult, I spent much time in hospitals undergoing more than a dozen surgeries, complicated by a heart condition, asthma, pneumonia, chronic bronchitis, and sudden deafness in one ear.

After making many mistakes throughout most of my earlier adult life, I adopted and integrated ten basic strategies for success. The strategies did not come to me all at once, but rather through a process as I began to determine what I really wanted in life. As I began to use these strategies one-by-one, I started to enjoy more success. By integrating the strategies, I have been able to exceed all of my previous goals and dreams. I have also enjoyed observing the success of other women I have trained and coached in incorporating these strategies into their lives.

This book is based on my experience and research, as well as on interviews with eighteen highly successful women. Although it is written for women who want to be successful in today's business world, it is also for women who want to be successful in life, regardless of their choices, goals, and experiences. Strategies, principles, and tips for success are integrated into the text to assist you in developing a personal action plan to achieve your goals and create success in your life.

Although most of the interviewees have done well financially and have not only survived but also thrived in a man's business world, they do not define success only in terms of financial income or career. They agree that success is different for each woman and that each of us needs to determine our own definition of success. The following definitions are samples from my conversations with these women:

- Success is a mental, physical, emotional, and spiritual balance in one's life.
- Success is being who one wants to be and doing what one wants to do.
- Success is feeling good about oneself.
- Success is making a contribution in this life and leaving a legacy for which one can be proud.
- Success is being able to fulfill our desires in all areas of life.
- Success is being able to determine one's own direction and to set one's own limits.
- Success is being able to do what God gave one the talents to do, based on what one has experienced and the lessons learned in doing so.

Although these definitions of success and the integration of the strategies in the following chapters apply to both women and men, this book is written primarily for women. If we were to measure success by monetary income alone, we would determine that women have made some progress since the passage of the Equal Pay Act in 1963; however, men's and women's salaries have yet to reach parity. Although the wage gap has narrowed since the Equal Pay Act was passed, American women's salaries still averaged only 76 percent of their male counterparts as recently as 1999. The average salary for women is lower than the average for men in more than 95 percent of occupations. Worldwide, women earn an average of 75 percent of the amount earned by men.

Financial income is only one measure of success, but it is an important one for most working women. For many of them, it also contributes to their feelings about success in other areas of their lives.

My purpose in writing this book is to assist women in creating success in their lives and in taking responsibility for their own success. In my experience of coaching both women and men, I have discovered that women are less likely to accept this responsibility, largely because they grew up with different paradigms. Many women who have worked in the business world believe that they need to behave like a man in order to be successful in business. I have proven in my own life that this is not the case. By using and integrating the strategies in this book, a woman can achieve success and still be a woman.

In addition to defining a new paradigm for success, in which measurement is based on your own definition of success rather than on the perceived expectations of others, *A Woman Can Do That!* will help you by doing the following:

- Giving strategies and examples on how to be successful both in business and in life.
- Assisting you to realize that success comes from within— and giving tips on how you can make this happen.
- Giving examples on how a woman can enjoy success, regardless of family background and experiences, limited educational background, economic status, the way she has been treated, and past mistakes.

- Showing that a woman can be successful in business without emulating male behavior.
- Demonstrating that success is available to each of us and that it is possible to be a winner without someone else having to lose.

The eighteen interviewees in this book have lived and worked in different parts of the world. They come from different backgrounds and have made different choices in their lives. They have made different mistakes and have overcome different obstacles. Yet, they subscribe to similar value systems and principles, which have been major factors in their success. In the following chapters, they share these values and principles in order to assist more women to enjoy success, as each of these eighteen women are now doing. During the interviews, the following women offered valuable tips and examples on the various strategies, which are described in the chapters ahead:

- **Nancy Albertini** (Dallas, Texas), founder, chairman of the board, and chief executive officer of Taylor Winfield, Inc., an executive search firm specializing in placing executives in technology businesses.

- **Lois Crandell** (San Diego, California), retired president and chief executive officer of Genetronics, a publicly traded medical device company; founder of two successful companies; featured in *Success* magazine.

- **Gayle Crowell** (San Francisco, California), member of seven corporate boards of directors including E.Piphany, currently the largest United States customer relationship management company; previously president and chief executive officer of Right Point, Inc., a large customer relationship management process and software company, which merged with E.Piphany in 1999.

- **Jeanne Elnadry, M.D.** (Yuma, Arizona), physician, specialist in internal medicine, and partner in a thriving medical practice.

- **Linda Herold** (Scottsdale, Arizona), publisher, "The Herold Report"; Fashion and Style editor, *Arizona Corridors* magazine; founder, Women of Scottsdale.

- **Beth MacDonald** (Manila, Philippines), regional franchise director for the Asia/Pacific Region for Johnson & Johnson.
- **Mollie Young Marinovich** (Edina, Minnesota), cofounding partner of Nametag International, Inc., an internationally recognized firm specializing in strategic brand development and naming.
- **Betty Notto** (Arden Hills, Minnesota), extremely successful homemaker and contributor to her community for fifty-five years.
- **Dee Ray** (Minneapolis, Minnesota), senior vice president and investment executive at John G. Kinnard & Company, an investment securities company; author of *Women, Money and Emotions.*
- **Wendy Franz Richards** (San Francisco, California), managing partner of MarTel Advisors, Inc., an investment and advisory services company; former director of the telecommunications practice at HSBC Investment Bank in London, England, and managing director, international business development, for AirTouch Europe (Vodafone AirTouch), based in the Netherlands and Belgium.
- **Laraine Rodgers** (Scottsdale, Arizona), vice president, Emerald Solutions, and former executive at Bell Atlantic Corporation, Xerox Corporation, American Express, and Citicorp/Citibank.
- **Joan T. Smith** (Minneapolis, Minnesota), retired vice president/ investment portfolio manager at Wells Fargo & Company (formerly Norwest Bank Minnesota); paved the way for women in this industry.
- **Bobbie Stevens, Ph.D.** (Naples, Florida), founder and president of Unlimited Futures, a human potential training company; author of *Unlimited Futures: How to Understand the Life You Have and Create the Life You Want.*
- **Terry Swack** (Boston, Massachusetts), vice president of experience design for Razorfish, a global digital services provider; previously founder and chief executive officer of TSDesign, an Internet strategy and product design firm with a customer base consisting of .com startups and Fortune 500 companies.
- **Charleen Tajiri** (Honolulu, Hawaii), founder and chief executive officer of Vision Health, a food supplement company which distributes its products through direct marketing channels; has

also reached the highest level of achievement in several multi-level marketing companies.

- **Kathy Brittain White, Ed.D.** (Dublin, Ohio), executive vice president and chief information officer at Cardinal Health, Inc.; former vice president of information systems at Allied Signal Corporation and associate professor at the University of North Carolina.

- **Laurie Windham** (San Francisco, California), founder, president and chief executive officer of Cognitiative, Inc., a San Francisco-based marketing, management, and consulting company; author of *Dead Ahead: The Web Dilemma and New Rules of Business* and *The Soul of the New Consumer: Attitudes, Behaviors, and Preferences of E-Customers.*

- **Constance B. "Connie" Wolf** (Scottsdale, Arizona), president of CBW, Inc., an organizational consulting and professional coaching company; previously European vice president of human resources and communications at Dow Corning.

These eighteen women have created success in their lives by using the strategies described in *A Woman Can Do That!* You can, too, if you are committed.

Each of the next ten chapters contains a separate strategy, along with instructions and/or suggestions on how to implement the strategy to create the success you want for yourself. As you read each chapter, you will engage in exercises or ponder some tips related to the strategy introduced in that chapter. You will also be integrating the strategy with those from previous chapters. Since each chapter builds on the strategies of previous chapters, I recommend that you read the chapters in sequence.

The strategies, as listed below, have the potential to change your life as you adopt and integrate them:

- Believe in Yourself!
- Dare to Dream!
- Determine Your Priorities!
- Set Powerful Goals!
- Ready—Aim—Take Action!

- Stay Focused!
- Remain Positive, No Matter What!
- Live Your Life with Integrity!
- Enjoy the Moment!
- Continue to Learn!

These strategies are simple, but they take some time to implement and integrate. Success is not instantaneous; rather, it is a process that requires commitment and work. The results are well worth the effort. Are you ready to create more success in your life? If so, turn the page, and let's get started!

CHAPTER

Believe in Yourself!

Developing self-confidence

Laurie Windham was destined to be a star. It seemed that she was born with an amazing talent—she started singing before she could walk or talk. She was an unusually gifted child and shared her talent by singing for relatives and friends while she was still in preschool. She enhanced her skills through countless hours of practice and, by the age of twelve, was performing in professional theater. She loved music and lived music. Her ultimate enjoyment in life was the time she spent performing. Because of her remarkable talent, the University of Texas granted her a voice scholarship.

A mezzo-soprano, Laurie sang a broad range of music including classical/opera, musical comedy and rock. Throughout adolescence and early adulthood she performed in musicals, including *Camelot*, *The Boyfriend*, and *Once Upon a Mattress*. She thoroughly enjoyed what she was doing and assumed that music would always be her profession and livelihood.

As a cheerleader in school, Laurie began to strain her voice. In addition, she suffered from chronic throat infections; nonetheless, she continued to sing, causing irreparable damage to her voice and throat. While she was in college, she had surgery to remove an abscess and scar tissue from her throat, thus leaving her unable to sing for over a year. She then attempted to continue her college studies in voice for the next two years, at which time the vocal performance professors at the University of Texas advised her that she did not have enough voice left to fulfill her dreams and aspirations.

"As you might expect," Laurie said, "this was a devastating blow. Up to that point in my life, I—and everyone who knew me—had defined me as a performer. I had never tried very hard in school to be good at anything else. I truly saw my career as being on the stage. When that was no longer an option, it created a serious identity crisis for me."

To salvage the college credits she had earned in music, Laurie changed her major from music to music therapy, a field that uses music as a therapeutic tool with disabled people. After working as a registered music therapist for four years, she began to evaluate alternative careers and decided to learn about the business world. She was soon accepted into the MBA program at Louisiana State University. Since she had not previously considered a career in business, Laurie knew that she had a challenge ahead of her. She rose to this challenge.

Today Laurie is president of a leading marketing and management consulting company in the San Francisco area. Her clients are mostly international companies, including Cisco Systems and Oracle Corporation. In addition to consulting, her company publishes a quarterly newsletter on e-business and funds ongoing customer research in that area. Laurie has written and published two books on e-business and is a sought-after speaker for conferences throughout the United States, Asia, and South America. She is an extremely successful woman, who has engineered that success herself.

Bobbie Stevens is another successful woman. Bobbie was a flight attendant for a major airline when she started wondering why some people were successful while others were not. She observed that true success did not seem to be related to education or IQ, but rather to the way people think. She began to study success and to experiment by creating thoughts that would create success in her life. As her experiment progressed, she became more and more excited about it—and she realized that she could create anything she wanted in her life.

As Bobbie engaged in her study, her initial goals were to buy a town house, a new car, new furniture, and a grand piano. Since a flight attendant's salary could not pay for all of this, she decided to become a real estate agent. She studied the real estate books, took the test, and received her real estate license. She then applied for a job for which she needed to take a battery of aptitude tests. When her future boss reviewed the test results with her, he said he was concerned about one of her answers. The question asked how much money she expected to make during her first year in real estate. She had answered this question by determining how much money she needed in order to pay for the town house, the car, the furniture, and the piano. He informed her that it had taken him five years of very hard work to make that much money. However, Bobbie knew that she could achieve this goal and left her answer unchanged. She developed and implemented an action plan for selling the amount of real estate needed to meet her objective. During her first year, she made exactly the amount of money she had predicted. Her earnings increased significantly each year she was in real estate.

Bobbie's success has continued to grow since her early days in real estate. She is currently president of Unlimited Futures, a company that specializes in helping people to realize their potential and to create their ideal life. She has developed an outstanding course for training others to use the methodology she has created and applied in order to enjoy success in life. Bobbie and her husband, Dean, who both are now Ph.D. psychologists, have trained thousands of people in this methodology and have seen their students significantly increase their success as a result of this course. Bobbie is the author of *Unlimited Futures: How to Understand the Life You Have and Create the Life You Want.*

Laurie Windham and Bobbie Stevens grew up in different parts of the United States. Their backgrounds and career choices are completely different. Neither came from a wealthy family. Neither is working in a career that she had even thought about as a child, in her teens, or even in her twenties. However, both are extremely successful, not only in their careers, but also in life.

One major characteristic that Laurie and Bobbie do share is the belief that they can *be*, *do* and *have* whatever they want in life. Each believes in herself and her ability to be successful. Each knows that she is capable of being the person she wants to be, and each has taken action based on this belief.

When asked to rate, on a five-point scale, the relationship of believing in oneself to success, all eighteen women interviewed for this book rated this a five, the highest rating possible. The interviewees agreed that success starts with this belief, or confidence, in oneself.

Many of us think that others have more self-confidence than we do—and that they are justified in feeling that way. After all, other people were born into families with more money, had a better chance for education, and had doting parents. Other women are prettier, they're taller, they're shorter, they're thinner, or they have better figures. They're married, they're single, or they have better behaved kids. Maybe their bosses like them better, or they are always in the right place at the right time.

I recently attended an interesting conference where Anita Roddick, founder of The Body Shop, was one of the keynote speakers. Anita, who started her business in Brighton, England, has built of chain of more than 600 cosmetics stores. When she walked onto the stage to deliver her keynote address, she exuded self-confidence. Many women in the audience later told me that, at that moment, they were wishing they could be more like her. Then she began to tell her story.

When she was a child, Anita knew that her family was different than most of the others in Littlehampton, England. Her family had moved to England from Italy when she was quite young. "We were noisy, always screaming and shouting," she said. "We played music loudly, ate pasta, and smelled of garlic." As a young woman, she lived a hippie lifestyle, married another hippie, and had two children.

Anita and her husband, Gordon, opened a restaurant and hotel, and they both worked hard to be successful in this business. They sold the restaurant a few years later when they realized that they were both physically and emotionally drained. Shortly thereafter, Gordon announced that he wanted to leave England for two years to ride a horse from Buenos Aires to New York. Because of their unusual relationship, Anita agreed. However, she would need to be doing some type of work to support their children for the next two years.

Anita decided that she would like to open "just a little shop" where she would sell cosmetics products made from natural ingredients and packaged in different-sized, inexpensive containers. From her past work experience in the restaurant and hotel, she was confident of her ability to think and work fast and to tweak her ideas until she had the right combination to get the results she wanted.

Although naysayers warned her about the potential for failure in the highly competitive cosmetics industry, Anita believed she could succeed. Her "little shop" has now grown into more than 600 stores worldwide. Anita started with an idea and a belief that she could succeed. *Inc.* magazine has since labeled her "the single force that has changed business forever."

The truth is that self-confidence is available to each of us. Every one of us has the ability to become a Laurie Windham, a Bobbie Stevens or an Anita Roddick. It doesn't matter where or when we were born. Our social background does not matter. Our financial background does not matter. It does not even matter if we have made huge mistakes in our lives. Each of us can develop the self-confidence needed to succeed. The following tips will help you to get started on this.

1. Think of yourself as the important person you are.

Many of us grow up believing that other people are more important than we are. There are many reasons for this. Some of us claim that we were conditioned to believe this way. Some of us think that we just were not given a fair chance in life. Some of us grow up with an inferiority complex, which we think is impossible to outgrow. Regardless of the reason, we just do not want to accept the possibility that we are as important as anyone else.

From the time I was fourteen years old, my goal was to become a computer programmer. Since this was during the early days of computers when there was no computer science curriculum, my plan was to major in mathematics in order to achieve my goal. However, at age nineteen I married a man who was deeply in debt. At that time, I had completed one year of college. In order to survive, I had to work full time and could not afford to continue my education. I accepted a position with the state of Minnesota and spent my days documenting accident reports and studying traffic patterns.

After almost two years, I was able to resume my education by taking night classes at the University of Minnesota while I worked full time during the day. In the next three years, I took every math, statistics, and computer class that was offered. I was excited one day when I learned that the State Civil Service Department was testing for a computer programmer position, which was to be filled within the next month. I saw this as an opportunity to meet my goal before I finished my college degree. I took the test and thought I had done well.

My heart was pounding as I opened the letter containing the test results. To my dismay, I had not received a passing score. When I shared the disappointing news with a colleague at work, he suggested that I go to the Civil Service office to review the test results. "I can't do that," I replied. "They're Civil Service, and they're always right." I was really saying that the person who sent out the test results knew more than I did, was more important than I was, and was not to be bothered by unimportant people like me.

Through some major coaxing and an offer to do the talking for me, my friend enticed me to go together with him to visit the Civil Service office. There I learned that the score for this test had been based on a combination of three criteria. The written test was fifty percent of the score, related education was forty percent, and length of state employment was ten percent. I had scored the highest score ever on the written test! I had been given five points for my five years of state employment. However, since the Civil Service Department had no record of my having attended college, my educational score was zero. Therefore, my total score was fifty-five percent. A score of seventy percent was needed to pass. With this new information, I was quickly able to transfer my college transcripts from the University of Minnesota to the State Civil Service Department, raising my total score by forty points. Within one week, I was offered the computer programmer position.

The rest of my life would have been different had I not visited the Civil Service office to inquire on the reason for my test score. Because I believed that other people were more important than I was, I didn't want to disturb them to inquire about something that meant even this much to me. Through this experience, I learned some valuable lessons. One of the main ones was that I am also an important person, but I needed to recognize this myself. Knowing this has opened many doors for me and, in turn, has contributed greatly to my success.

Dr. Dennis Deaton, who is one of my favorite authors and speakers, teaches that "you alter your destiny by altering your thoughts." How true this has been in my life! The more I think of myself as successful, the more successful I become. This is also true for all eighteen women interviewed for this book. It will also be true for you.

2. Practice daily personal affirmations.

In order to believe in yourself, you need to train your subconscious mind. Many of us have conditioned our subconscious minds in the past to believe that we are less than what we are. The subconscious mind does not think for itself; therefore, it believes whatever is fed into it. If it hears negative comments, it believes them. If it hears positive comments, it believes them. Unfortunately, most of us hear, and pay attention to, many more negative comments than positive ones. This is why positive affirmations are so necessary. All of us need to train and retrain our subconscious minds by assuring that they are fed positive thoughts. The subconscious mind does not think, reason, or create. It merely reacts to the thoughts of the conscious mind.

The conscious mind dominates the subconscious mind with dominant thought. World-renowned motivational speaker Earl Nightingale said, "We must control our thinking. The same rule that can lead us to a life of success, wealth, happiness and all the things we have ever dreamed of . . . that very same law can lead us into the gutter."

In *The Intuitive Manager*, author Roy Rowen writes, "Male or female, top brass or lowly trainee, the decision-maker needs to understand how the brain constantly delves into the subconscious to retrieve buried fragments of knowledge and experience, which it then instantaneously fuses with new information."

In *Brain Building*, Marilyn vos Savant, says, "Just as the human body can be strengthened and toned to muscular power through . . . exercise, so too can the mind be strengthened and sharpened. You can't build a great body in a few hours; the same goes for your intellect. Remember that the secret to the success of any exercise program is repetition, repetition, repetition. Only then will you begin to see results."

The subconscious mind can be your ally in building your self-confidence. It can help you to believe in yourself, to believe in your abilities and your potential. But you need to train the subconscious mind and to be diligent in this training. Repeated affirmations, over an extended period of time, will contribute greatly to this training.

I once participated in a class where the students were asked to select three adjectives that would describe themselves. We were instructed to not think or reason, but just to recite the first three positive adjectives that came into our heads. The first three adjectives that entered my mind were "confident, committed, and powerful." I doubt whether the adjectives would have been the same back in the days when I needed to be coerced to visit the Civil Service office to review my test results. I had come a long way since then, but I still didn't realize that I thought of myself as confident and powerful. As I reflected on these words, I knew that they were true; however, I needed to keep reminding my subconscious of this. I began, several times each day, to repeat the phrase, "I am a confident, committed, powerful woman." I repeated it to myself whenever I was to give a presentation to a large group, whenever I was walking into a meeting with our company's top management, whenever I needed to handle a difficult employee situation, and whenever I was in a situation where I might have previously lacked confidence. I repeated it when I was driving in traffic, as I waited in a supermarket line, when I woke up in the morning, and when I went to bed at night. Because my subconscious mind heard this phrase so often, it became part of my personal belief system. The phrase "I am a confident, committed, powerful woman" has helped me to enjoy more success than I had previously thought possible. I still think of myself with these three adjectives, plus one other—"caring." To this date, I often remind myself that I am a confident, committed, powerful, caring woman.

Each woman needs to determine for herself the affirmations that she wants to use. Following are some examples that women have shared with me:

- I am a successful woman.
- I have greatness in me.
- I am creating and achieving my dreams.
- I am talented and am using these talents for good.
- I am terrific!

Your affirmations do not have to be long. In fact, shorter ones tend to be easier to remember. You'll want to have some that relate to your personal goals in life. Notice that the above affirmations all are in the present tense. This is important, because the subconscious mind operates only in the present.

It is important to recite your affirmations to yourself several times each day. As you do this, you will be training your subconscious mind. Dr. Napoleon Hill, author of *Think and Grow Rich*, said, "Whatever the mind can conceive and believe, the mind can achieve."

3. Emulate self-confident people.

Who is it you admire most? Most likely, this person possesses much self-confidence. Is this person a woman or a man? Either way, you might want to think about the characteristics of this person who you may want to emulate. Regardless of who this person is, you can be selective in the characteristics you choose. If this person happens to be a man, I want you to know that you do not need to behave like a man in order to be successful. (I'm living proof of this.) You do not need to behave like another woman, either.

Each and every one of us has the freedom to select characteristics of those whom we admire and to emulate only the characteristics we select. We can learn much by observing self-confident women. How do they dress? How do they walk and talk? What is their posture? When do they stand? When do they sit? How do they enter a conversation? How do they start a conversation?

Other ways to learn to emulate the characteristics we admire in self-confident, successful people are to talk with them and to ask for their advice. Most people love to hear that others admire them, and they enjoy sharing their wisdom, experience, and advice. A caution, however, is to consciously listen to what they have to say and be willing to take action based on the advice we request.

As you continue to observe self-confident people, you might want to make a list of the characteristics that you most admire about each person. You can then form a list of characteristics you most want to emulate. These would be the characteristics that would help you most in enhancing your self-confidence. The next step would be to determine how you are going to integrate these characteristics into your own personal style. Again, remember that you do not need to be exactly like someone else to be a confident, successful person. The beauty of this is that we can each have our own style and still enjoy all the success we desire in life.

4. Reward yourself for each success.

In a world where we have been raised to be modest and to not "blow our own horns," it is often difficult to accept praise or even to admit that we are successful. How often have you complimented someone on an achievement and received a response such as, "Oh, it was nothing"?

When I told my interviewees that I considered them to be successful, I followed up by asking if they agreed with my statement. All eighteen women agreed. If they hadn't, the interview would have ended at that point. In order to be successful, a woman needs to have enough self-confidence to admit to others that she is successful. This does not mean that she needs to brag about this. It just means that she recognizes herself for this success.

Recognition contributes to self-confidence, and we can't depend on others to give us this recognition. Genuine success comes from within. It is self-generated. It is the realization that we are accomplishing our goals and our mission in life. Each of us measures our own success on our own yardstick. As we do this, we need to generate our own recognition.

As we give recognition to ourselves for our accomplishments, we expand our enthusiasm and energy to accomplish more. As we are recognized, our self-confidence grows. Self-confidence breeds more self-confidence, which breeds more success. As we continue to reward ourselves for our successes, the cycle continues.

The type of success you reward is up to you. I can reward myself for writing five pages of this book by taking a break to go for a walk in the park, by treating myself to an ice cream cone, or by making a phone call to a friend. When I finish a chapter, I might celebrate by going out to dinner or to the theater with my husband.

When the book is published and has sold a million copies, I will plan a trip to Rome and Florence.

The type of reward is also up to you. It might be as simple as a soak in the tub or giving yourself permission to jump up and click your heels together. What is important is that you recognize yourself for achieving a goal. As you recognize yourself more, you will achieve more goals, and your confidence in yourself will grow.

5. Surround yourself with positive people.

My former secretary, Lisa, is one of the most positive, enthusiastic, self-confident people I know. Although she is still quite young, she knows exactly what she wants at this point in her life, and she gets it. I met Lisa when I accepted an assignment to form a new department at 3M. At that time, Lisa was in a department that was being outsourced, and she was looking for a job. She was one of seventeen employees who applied for one of the four secretarial positions in my new department. She had never been a secretary before, but she was confident that she could do the job. Because of Lisa's attitude, I decided to take a chance on her and hired her as my own secretary. We worked together for more than three years, and she continued to amaze me with her attitude. Her enthusiasm was contagious within the department. She also became an excellent secretary. During a performance review meeting, I commented on Lisa's positive attitude and asked how she had developed it. She replied, "When I was growing up, my mother never criticized me."

Olympic champion Wilma Rudolph was the twentieth of the twenty-two children in her family. Weak and frail as a child, she contracted pneumonia, scarlet fever, and polio. As a result, her doctors had little hope that she would ever be able to walk. With the encouragement of her mother, Wilma worked at taking one step and then another until, at age eleven, she was able to make it from one side of her yard to the other. When she started high school, she made the basketball team and became one of the starting players when she was a senior. With much hard work, determination, and more encouragement from her mother, she continued to improve her athletic abilities. At the Rome Olympic Games in 1960, she won three gold medals, set world records in both the one-hundred-meter dash and the two-hundred-meter dash, and ran the anchor leg in the 4X100-meter relay. She was called the fastest woman on earth. When asked how she had overcome her disability, she responded, "The doctors said I would never walk. My mother said I would. I believed my mother."

Not all of us have had the opportunity to live most of our life with positive people, with people who encourage us, with people who do not criticize us. Later in this book, you will meet Linda Herold, another woman who has created success in her life. Linda said, "For me, the love of life, love of people, and love of beauty developed over time. Having been an unloved child, I had to decide for myself what life would be like. Accepting that I was alone in the world early on forced me to look inside, always asking what do I want and how can I achieve it. It also helped me to feel compassion for others who feel the same loss of love." Linda selected friends who were positive and supportive. She surrounded herself with people who loved life and loved people. She disassociated herself from negative people. Today she says, "With patience and perseverance, I have been rewarded with an ample share of love, joy, beauty and companionship."

Have you ever noticed the group dynamics when one person in the group makes a negative statement and another person adds to this negativity? At this point, it is tempting for the others in the group to become negative. The next time this happens in your life, you might want to think about how you feel during this conversation and afterward. Then contrast these feelings with the ones that you have during and after a positive conversation. You will definitely notice a difference. You will feel much better during and after the positive conversations.

As you include more positive people in your circle of friends, you yourself will become more positive. As you become more positive, you will attract more positive people. As you attract more positive people into your life, your self-confidence will grow. As your self-confidence grows, others will also have more confidence in you.

6. Look and feel your best.

Many women have told me they would feel better about themselves if they were better looking or had a better-shaped body. They feel their nose is too large, their hair is too thin or their feet are too big.

The truth is that very few people in this world have beautiful faces and perfect bodies, and many women who do have beautiful faces and perfect bodies also have a poor self-image. The difference, for many of us, is that we feel better about ourselves when we look our best. Following are some tips from successful women on looking and feeling your best:

- Wear clothes that are appropriate for the occasion. These clothes do not have to be expensive, but they should fit well and be clean and pressed.
- Practice good grooming habits at all times.
- Have your hair styled to look best for you.
- If you think you look better with makeup, wear makeup every day, even if the only person to see you is yourself when you look in the mirror.
- Stand and sit straight.
- Get enough sleep to look and feel good. Most women need eight hours of sleep each night. Some will get by with six, and others will need nine or more. Let your body tell you how much sleep you need, and make this a priority.
- Maintain good health. See your doctor when you are ill, and have regular physical checkups.
- Stay physically fit. Aerobic exercises will help, especially walking and swimming.
- Wear a smile. You will soon notice that this will help to attract more positive people into your life. Smiles are contagious. When you smile at others, you'll find that many of them will also smile at you.

The better you look, the better you'll feel about yourself. Most people who practice these simple tips for two weeks begin to notice a difference. As people notice a difference, they make a habit of practicing these tips. As the habits are formed, self-confidence increases.

7. Fake it until you make it.

This is the only place in this book where you will be advised to fake anything. Personal integrity is most important to me, and I believe that honesty is critical to success. What I am recommending here is that you act the part of the woman who believes in herself. By acting self-confident, most women begin to realize that they can be self-confident.

I once took a class to help build my self-confidence. One class exercise was to go to a shopping mall, introduce yourself to a stranger, and engage in a conversation with this stranger. Sales personnel in the mall did not count for points. If we were able to dine with the stranger, we were given extra credit. Since I was quite shy at the time, this was an extremely scary challenge for me. I hesitated and procrastinated. Finally, when I had just one hour left before I had to be back in class, I went into a fast food restaurant within the mall. I ordered my food and looked for a friendly looking, lone female customer. When I finally spotted her, I noticed an empty table next to hers. I stood tall while waiting for my food, walked tall to the empty table, and sat tall once I arrived at the table. It was good to sit down, because my knees were shaking. I looked at her, smiled, and asked a question about one of the stores in the mall. Fortunately, she carried the ball from there. She seemed to have a lot of self-confidence. I acted like I did, also. I moved to her table and got the extra points, but I learned that the points for doing this were worth much less than the lesson that I learned and the friend that I gained that day.

Sometimes we have to put ourselves into uncomfortable situations in order to gain confidence in ourselves. When I started working for 3M, my top fear was the fact that I might have to speak in public at some time. Research indicates that this is the number one fear for people in general. I knew that, in order to achieve my goals,

I would need to become a good public speaker. This was a paradox for me. To overcome this fear, I joined a Toastmistress Club. My first speech was just seven minutes long. It was about myself, a topic that required no research. I practiced until I could deliver this speech flawlessly. When it came time to give the speech, I consciously tried to demonstrate self-confidence; however, my knees shook, and my voice sounded like I was crying. I didn't remember ever before having been as nervous as I was when I gave this speech. However, I tried to demonstrate all of the self-confidence I thought I lacked. As I gave more speeches, my confidence grew to the point that public speaking soon became one of my favorite things to do.

If a woman thinks of herself as successful, she is successful. If she believes in herself, others will also believe in her. The reverse is also true. By demonstrating self-confidence, even when she doesn't think she has it, she will become more self-confident.

8. Affirm those around you.

There are not many people in the world who can't benefit from more self-confidence. I have learned that even the most arrogant and seemingly self-assured people often lack the inner confidence needed to really feel good about themselves. Even these people need compliments. However, when affirming and complimenting people, it is important to be genuine and honest.

The universe is connected. It took me many years to appreciate the saying, "What goes around, comes around." If we are looking for recognition and confidence, we need to recognize and have confidence in others. In business, the most confident executives and managers I know are the ones who give credit to their people who do the work. In life, the most confident people are the ones who demonstrate confidence in others.

When I interviewed Rita for a management position a few years ago, I found myself wishing more people could be like her. She exhibited more self-confidence than almost anyone would feel in this type of situation. When she walked into my office, she created a good first impression even before any words were spoken. Her posture was erect, her grooming was impeccable, and she was dressed appropriately and professionally. She was well prepared for the interview, answering my questions with much knowledge and professionalism. She also asked some good questions herself. At the end of the interview, she referred to some notes and told me that the information I had given her fit the criteria she had specified for her next job. She reviewed these criteria with me, along with her qualifications for the position. Although I had scheduled eleven additional interviews for this position, I knew immediately that Rita, who was the first interviewee, would be a top candidate.

A year after Rita moved to my department, I sponsored a "power goaling" workshop for all employees in the department. Rita was eager to review her power goal with me the following week. Once again, she was aspiring to greatness and had developed an action plan to achieve her next major goal in life. To my surprise, she had some questions regarding her potential to reach this goal. Because she shared these concerns with me, I shared with her my own prior experiences with low self-confidence and gave her some suggestions for moving forward.

The next day, Rita hand-delivered to my office a thank you note that I will cherish forever. In the note, she had written, "Thank you very much for the insight you provided yesterday by sharing your story. There are so many mini-lessons I learned that have been running through my mind, especially that confidence can be learned!"

Indeed, confidence can be learned. Self-esteem can be developed. The first step is to believe in yourself. I had learned this lesson and was able to convey it to Rita and to others. My goal is that you, too, will benefit from our experience.

The proverb, "As a man thinketh in his heart, so is he" can also be stated, "As a woman thinketh in her heart, so is she."

CHAPTER

Dare to Dream!

Visualizing your reality

"We alter our destiny by altering our thoughts," Dr. Dennis Deaton stated emphatically as he stood in front of his audience of more than 100 students and looked directly at me. "If we will master the power of our minds, we may do or be whatsoever we will." It was February 1994, and I was attending the course on Visioneering that Dr. Deaton had developed and taught through the human potential development company that he had founded. I had learned about the power of visualization two years earlier, and I was convinced that it had been a strong factor in putting me on the fast track to creating an ideal life for myself. I decided that now was the time to speed up the pace.

Using the Visioneering process, which includes visualizing sensory-rich, emotion-laden images, I began to create my next position at 3M through visualization. I had often said that I would like to have an international assignment, to have the opportunity to live and work outside of the United States. By this time, I knew that just talking about it was not going to make it happen. I needed to start things moving by visualizing my desires, then putting these desires in pictures that my subconscious could understand in order for it to begin its work. I later wrote the following description of this initial visualization:

> On Saturday, October 1, 1994, I see my husband, Cliff, and I arriving in our new red Audi 100 at the home we have selected in Brussels, Belgium, where we will be living for the next two years. This is the beginning of my new assignment as 3M's European sales and marketing productivity manager, a position that I have worked toward for the past eleven years.
>
> It is a warm autumn day. The sun is shining brightly in the clear blue sky, and the leaves on the trees have started to turn red and gold. In front of us is our new home, which is brown brick with white trim and has a pointed roof. Its two-car garage is waiting for the Audi, which is a company car, and also for the second car that we will purchase later this month.
>
> I am excited about this excellent opportunity to not only increase the company's sales and marketing effectiveness in Europe and enhance my career, but also to see and experience much of Europe, including the Vatican and the Leaning Tower of Pisa in Italy, the Eiffel Tower and the Louvre in Paris, the theater in London, the green rolling landscape of Ireland, the Alps, ancient cathedrals and museums.
>
> Cliff and I look forward to making new acquaintances with the many Europeans that we will meet in the next two years. We are also eager to host many of our American friends and relatives in Europe.

I repeated the visualization process at least twice each day for several weeks. As I did this, the vision expanded to include the sounds of people speaking English in different accents. It also included aromas, such as those of Belgian waffles and French perfume. As I was able to see my goals more clearly, the original vision was altered until it reached the point where I knew it was what I really wanted. The rest was easy. My vision became a reality before the end of the year. The fantastic results of this visualization process are described later in this chapter. First, let's review the results of several other visualizations, the steps in the visualization process, and how visualization can contribute to your success.

I had first practiced visualization two years earlier while participating in a course facilitated by Dr. Dean Portinga. The course had been developed by his wife, Dr. Bobbie Stevens, who had developed a process for creating an ideal life for herself. Dr. Stevens and Dr. Portinga (or Bobbie and Dean, as they prefer to be called) had founded Unlimited Futures, a company that provides programs for the development of human potential for both individuals and corporations. Bobbie, who we met in Chapter 1, had come to the realization that there are some basic principles of life that govern all that is created. One of these principles is that mental energy directs physical energy. "This is how we create experiences in our lives," she says. "We create our own experiences through our own thoughts or, more accurately, through our deepest beliefs."

Dennis Deaton agrees with this. In *The Book on Mind Management*, he writes, "We think, and with those thoughts, we create. We create the world we live in. It goes beyond influencing, shaping, or guiding. You and I, in very literal terms, determine what we experience and what we enact into the world. We establish our own happiness or misery, abundance or scarcity . . . We harvest in life, only and exactly, what we sow in our minds."

Bobbie Stevens, who has the same understanding, was sure that she could create whatever she desired in her life. She began by experimenting at the material level. She visualized the town house, car, and piano that she wanted to own. She also visualized her job selling real estate to pay for these things. She truly believed that these things would manifest in her life, and they did. She went on to visualize bigger and better material things, and they all manifested. When I met Bobbie, she and her husband owned and lived in a fabulous 7,000-square-foot house, which was on a lake and had a waterfall and trees in the foyer, a swimming pool, and a tennis court.

In themselves, the material things were nice to have, but Bobbie did not stop at that. There were nonmaterial things that were much more important to her. She visualized some higher education and now has two doctorates. She visualized a strong spirituality, and she and her husband now teach spirituality courses throughout the United States. Perhaps the most important of her visualizations was when she decided to use the process to attract someone into her life that would be perfectly suited to her in every way.

"If he was perfectly suited for a relationship with me, where we could share our work and life together, what would he be like?" she asked herself. "First, he would have some knowledge about the kinds of things I am now working with, plus a strong interest in this field. He should probably be a psychologist. It would also be good if he had some business background. Of course, he would be intelligent and good-looking. He would also be fun to be with. I can get pretty focused on work, so he should like fun things in order to help me stay light. He would also be curious, an explorer. He would enjoy handling some details, like vacations. He would be very supportive and easy to live with. He would be thoughtful and considerate. We would love each other deeply, and he would appreciate me for being who I am. It would be a very special relationship, and everyone we meet would be inspired by it."

Bobbie worked on enhancing her vision and knew that it would manifest in time. And, it did. A short time later, she met Dean Portinga, exactly the man she had described, at a retreat. They have been married for more than twenty years and have shared the process of visualization with thousands of students. They are an example of what they teach, and their relationship is indeed inspiring.

At the time I participated in Bobbie and Dean's course, I had been dating Cliff for about ten months. I knew I loved Cliff, and I enjoyed his company. However, the relationship seemed like it was not going anywhere. Cliff had had a heart attack shortly after I met him, and I lived in fear that I might lose him someday. I had a good management position at 3M, but it also seemed that my career had become stagnant. I had a good life, but I wanted it to be better and didn't know how to make it better.

When a business associate mentioned that Bobbie and Dean's course was the best he had ever taken, I was eager to learn more about it. Cliff and I both attended an orientation to learn more about the course. During the orientation, my dominant left brain kept telling me that this is crazy, and it won't work. However, it was evident what the process had done for Bobbie and Dean, and they seemed like such sincere people. Also, my associate, who recommended the course, was a left-brain person, much like myself. My biggest surprise was that Cliff believed everything that Bobbie and Dean were saying. Because he is a chiropractor, he understood completely how mental energy directs physical energy. After a week of discussion, we both decided to participate in the course.

In the beginning of the course, I was still very skeptical. I think Dean could perceive this when he started with a quote from Albert Einstein, "Imagination is more important than knowledge." I decided that, if this was good enough for Albert Einstein, it was good enough for me. I would, at least, pay attention.

Before the first visualization exercise, Dean asked us to write seven choices we would like to manifest in our lives, starting with the words, "I choose." I wrote the following:
1. I choose to sell my house and build my dream home.
2. I choose to own a new Lexus or Acura.
3. I choose friendships with enthusiastic, energetic, intelligent, caring people.
4. I choose a close relationship with a caring husband, who is my soul mate.
5. I choose closer relationships with my children.
6. I choose to be promoted at work into a position having more responsibility.
7. I choose to be more spiritual and more caring.

Our next step was to close our eyes and visualize what each of these choices would look like in our lives, but we didn't stop there. We learned that visualization works best when we act as if our vision has already happened. We went back to our seven choices and changed "I choose" to "I have." Visualization was difficult for me at first, but it began to get easier as I did it more often. Of these original seven choices, I was able to manifest the following in my life:

1. I have sold my house and am building my dream home.
At the time I participated in this course, my house had been for sale for several months, and I had received no offers. I had bought a lot on a beautiful pond, and I needed to sell my house in order to start building. I visualized an immediate sale of my home to cash buyers who wanted to close and move in immediately. The following week, I received a cash offer! The buyers wanted to close in nine days and to move in on the day of closing. This was my first experience with visualization, and it was almost spooky! I put most of my belongings in storage and moved to an apartment temporarily while the dream home was being built.

2. I have a new Lexus or Acura.
This one was easy. I currently have an Acura RL. It is a beautiful car.

3. I have friendships with enthusiastic, energetic, intelligent, caring people.
I am particularly blessed in this area. This world is full of beautiful people, many of whom are my closest friends. Each year, I am fortunate to expand my circle of friends as I meet more enthusiastic, energetic, intelligent, caring people.

4. I have a close relationship with a caring husband, who is my soul mate.
Cliff and I were able to open up to the class and share our feelings about each other. I felt he was avoiding me at times. He thought I worried too much. I admitted that I had a fear of him having another heart attack. Dean suggested that we all visualize Cliff as being healthy. I found that when I visualized Cliff as being healthy, it eliminated my fears. When I stopped worrying, he stopped avoiding me. Our relationship began to grow closer. He proposed later

that year. We have an excellent marriage, one that I would not have dreamed possible before I started taking charge of my dreams and visions.

5. I have closer relationships with my children.

At the time, my son, Bryan, was twenty-five and my daughter, Shelley, was nineteen. We were close, but I thought that we could be closer. As time goes on, the three of us continue to be a close family. This was exemplified at a recent party that 3M gave in my honor. Shelley asked the party planners if she could speak during the program portion of the celebration. She gave a tribute that would cause any mother to beam with pride. She ended by saying, "She is not only my mother. She is my friend, confidant, and mentor." Afterward, Bryan told his grandmother that he was so proud of his sister that it brought tears to his eyes.

6. I have been promoted at work into a position having more responsibility.

Three months later, a new vice president transferred into my business unit. I immediately wrote him a letter describing the position I had created during the visualization process. Within a month, he appointed me to this position. I received three additional promotions in the next five years.

7. I am more spiritual and more caring.

This is one that I continue to work on. Spirituality is extremely important to me. People are extremely important to me. I pray every night that I will remember this in everything I do the following day.

Visualization was one of the critical steps in the process taught in this course. By the time I completed the course, I felt like I was walking on clouds. I was a firm believer in the power of visualization.

Do you engage in visualization? Of course, you have dreams. I have never met a person without dreams. But do you have a structured program to make these dreams come true? Walt Disney said, "If you can dream it, you can do it."

Henry David Thoreau said, "If one advances confidently in the direction of [her] dreams, and endeavors to live the life which [she] has imagined, [she] will meet with success unexpected in common hours." Dee Ray is a woman who has advanced confidently in the direction of her dreams and has met with success. Her success may have been unexpected by others who knew her and her background.

She was born in a small town in Wisconsin and was raised with six brothers and sisters in a house that had no indoor plumbing. To Dee, the land of opportunity could have seemed too far away to even try to find it. However, she is now senior vice president of a regional investment company. She has been awarded several high distinctions and has been featured in many newspaper and magazine articles for her success in investment counseling.

The road to success, starting in the early-1960s, was not easy for Dee. When she started her career, most women in business were secretaries. After performing secretarial duties for a period of time and excelling at these responsibilities, Dee decided that she wanted to be a stockbroker. She spent her evenings studying. Although she passed the stockbroker test with high scores, the brokerage firm for which she worked had a policy that all stockbrokers had to be men. The unstoppable Dee Ray found a brokerage firm that would admit women stockbrokers, and she has since become one of the most successful women in this field.

Dee was determined, and she possessed a strong work ethic. She was also a visionary and stuck with her vision of becoming a highly successful stockbroker. She later read books by some of the experts in visualization and began to practice the things that she learned from these books. As she practiced, she became more and more successful.

One of Dee's favorite books is *Psycho-Cybernetics* by Dr. Maxwell Maltz, in which he wrote, "The creative mechanism within you is impersonal. It will work automatically and impersonally to achieve goals which you yourself set for it. Present it with success goals, and it functions as a success mechanism. Present it with negative goals, and it operates just as impersonally and just as faithfully as a failure mechanism."

Dee visualizes success, not only for herself, but also for her clients. Her personal mission is to create wealth for her clients. "I don't pay any attention to the commission rates for the different [financial] products," she stated. "I just recommend the products that will help each individual meet his or her goals." As a result, she also benefits.

In *You'll See It When You Believe It*, Dr. Wayne Dyer says, "Your determination to succeed is nothing more than your thought to do so. The idea of success is really the thought of success." In this book, he shares that his thoughts had always created his world. He described his visualization process at age thirteen. He spent many nights watching *The Tonight Show* on a tiny black-and-white television. He pictured himself as a guest on *The Tonight Show* and, in his mind, practiced talking with the host, Steve Allen. He would actually work on routines, as he imagined himself being a guest on the show. In his mind's picture, he was an adult appearing on the show and discussing the things he knew to be true. Even then, he visualized himself telling *The Tonight Show* audience that we are able to choose our own destinies.

Dr. Dyer wrote *Your Erroneous Zones* while he was teaching at a university. He struggled for almost a year with the thought that he needed to go out on his own and leave the security of a bimonthly paycheck. "I had wonderful pictures in my mind's eye," he said. "I saw myself talking to everyone in America about the ideas I had just finished writing about in *Your Erroneous Zones*. I could see in my mind that the book was going to be very successful." He left his university position and began working his plan to follow his dreams. As negative people told him that he could not accomplish his vision, he became even more committed.

A year later, his book was on the *New York Times* best-seller list. His vision had begun to manifest! Soon the book was at the top of the list, where it stayed for almost two years. One day, he received the "magic phone call" that was to lead to the fulfillment of the image that he had had since he was thirteen years old. He appeared on *The Tonight Show* three times in an eleven-day period.

In *You'll See It When You Believe It*, he states, "[*Your Erroneous Zones*] was eventually published in twenty-six languages around the world. Other books have followed, as have tapes, articles, international travel for professional speaking engagements, and an opportunity for me to make a difference in the lives of millions and millions of people. I received more money in the first year I was on my own without the security of a regular paycheck than I had in the entire thirty-six years of my life before then."

Visualization is not new. It has been used since the beginning of time. Aristotle said that the soul cannot think without pictures. "The reasoning mind thinks in the form of images. . . . As the mind determines the objects it should pursue or avoid in terms of these images, even in the absence of sensation, it is stimulated to action when occupied with them."

In more recent times, Conrad Hilton created mental pictures of owning a hotel before having one. Ray Kroc, the founder of McDonald's, wrote in *Grinding It Out: The Making of McDonald's* that he used mental images to create his goals. Visualization is the most widely used mental tool in modern sports. Mike Powell, world record holder in the long jump, would picture his record jump as he would jump from his kitchen through the dining room into the den over the green shag carpeting and land in front of his mother's red leather easy chair. He was in second place in Tokyo when his vision came back to him. He later said, "As I stare at the horizon, at the peak of my jump, I think I see, just for a second, my mom's red leather easy chair at the end of the pit."

Lois Crandell, who recently retired from her position as chief executive officer of a large San Diego-based medical device company, knew the meaning of struggle and hardship as a child. The oldest of ten children, she grew up on a farm in rural Minnesota. When she was three years old, her younger sister died in a fire that destroyed their farmhouse. Her mother, who had been burned over eighty percent of her body, spent several months in the hospital before she recovered and returned to her family.

Lois had many chores on the farm, which included cooking for the family at age eight, driving a tractor by the age of nine, and helping with the younger siblings. She dreamed of living by the ocean. While reading *The Strangest Secret* by Earl Nightingale, she realized how important visualization would be in order to make this dream come true. She read the words, "We must control our thinking. The same rule that can lead us to a life of success, wealth, happiness and all the things we have ever dreamed of . . . that very same law can lead us into the gutter. It's all in how we use it . . . for good or for bad. This is the strangest secret in the world."

After reading about visualization and success, Lois wrote ten goals and visualized the achievement of these goals each day for a year. She has achieved all ten of these goals, which included an excellent marital relationship, running a venture company and taking it public, and living in California. As she visualized, she thought of Earl Nightingale's statement about a person becoming what she thinks about. "When I would close my eyes and see these visualization scenarios, I would actually see the Pacific Ocean from a dwelling high above it," she said. "I now live in a condo, which overlooks Mission Bay. On a clear day, I can see the Pacific Ocean. As I sit in my favorite spot, that old visualization from more than ten years ago comes back to me."

Mollie Young Marinovich is another extremely successful woman who practices visualization. Mollie is cofounding partner of Nametag International, Inc., an internationally recognized firm specializing in strategic brand development and naming. Her company, which has two offices in the United States and one in Europe, has been featured as brand experts in many national publications, including *Wall Street Journal*, *Life* magazine, *American Demographics*, and *Success*. Nametag was recently named as one of the top thirty emerging companies by a leading Midwestern business publication. In the early days before her business was doing well, "I would sit at my desk and create mental pictures of the success of the business," she said.

Lois and Mollie are strong believers in the power of visualization. So is Arnold Schwarzenegger, who oncesaid, "The key to success is to create a vision of who you want to be, and then picture it as if it has already happened." In 1976, a sports reporter asked Arnold what he was going to do, now that he had retired from bodybuilding. The reporter was startled by the answer. "I am going to be the number-one-box-office star in all of Hollywood," Arnold said. As the reporter wondered how this man with the thick Austrian accent and monstrous build could become a box-office star, Arnold explained that he would use the same visualization process that helped him to become very successful at bodybuilding. Arnold had created his vision of being a very successful actor, just as he had created his vision of being a very successful bodybuilder. The rest is history.

Are you visualizing your success? If so, great! If not, let's get started. Now that you've read some examples of how visualization has affected the lives of successful people, it's time to make this process work for you. As you learn more about the visualization process from different authors and/or seminars, you will see that the steps in the process can vary. Although you will want to use the process that works best for you, it's important to remember that each of the various processes focuses on creating mental pictures in the *present tense*. The following process has created success for me in business and in life.

1. Determine what you want to create in your life.

What do you really want in life? What does success mean to you? What will you commit to achieving? We'll spend more time clarifying your desires in a later chapter, but now you should have an idea of what you would like to create in your life. When determining this, be sure to take into consideration all aspects of your life. Include such factors as relationships, health, career, material wants and needs, spiritual growth, and anything else that is important to you. Make a written list of these things. Be sure to write the *result* of what you wish to create, not *how* you plan to get it. Read your list to make sure that these are the things you want to create. Lois Crandell says, "Be careful what you visualize, because you will get it!"

Next, review your list to make sure that it is in the present tense. When you visualize, your subconscious mind will be working in the present tense. Also, make sure that you have written what you want, not what you don't want. When you visualize, you'll need to concentrate on what you want. For example, if you are overweight, don't write that you want to lose weight. Your subconscious mind will focus on the word *weight*, rather than the fact that you want a thinner, healthier, more-attractive body. In this case, you might want to write, "I am physically healthy and attractive."

Now review your list again. Have you written the desired results of what you want to create, rather than how you will create it? Are the items on the list in the present tense? Are the items stated as the results you want, rather than as the results you don't want? Are they really what you want, rather than the things you think you should want? Do all of the items on your list excite you? Cross out the ones that do not excite you.

By now, you have probably written, crossed out, and rewritten several of the items on your list. Look at the list one more time. Are you making choices for other people in any of the items on your list? If so, you will want to reword these. For example, you can choose the kind of relationship you want, but don't name the other person in that relationship. That person will need to make his or her own choices. Ensure that none of the items conflict with each other. Also, you will want to make sure that the items on your list do not cause harmful effects to another person.

2. Eliminate distractions.

Distractions come in two varieties: internal and external. You can have control over both. First, you will want to eliminate the external distractions. Go to a quiet place where you will not be interrupted. Some people have the advantage of a convenient, serene forest, lakeside, or mountain setting. For others, it might be an office, a bedroom, or even a closet. If there is a telephone in the room, turn off the ringer. If you have a pager or a cell phone, turn it off.

The internal distractions are more difficult for most of us to eliminate, but it can be done. We all have so many things on our minds that our thoughts will tend to wander if we do not discipline our minds to stay focused on the task at hand. I recommend engaging in the visualization process while in a sitting position. Most of us can relax while we are sitting, and we're more likely to stay awake when we're sitting rather than lying down.

Close your eyes and give yourself some time to unwind. If your mind wanders onto a trivial matter and you think you must remember it, open your eyes and write it down. Then close your eyes again, stay seated, and unwind.

3. Relax your body and your mind.

Most of us do not realize how much stress and tension is in our body until we start to relax. If you have a favorite relaxation technique, use it now to relax your body before you start visualizing. If you do not have a favorite technique, I would suggest the following, which works well for me:

- Now that you are in a sitting position with your eyes closed, let the chair support your body.
- Uncross your legs and feel yourself sink into the chair.
- Take a deep breath, inhaling slowly. Hold your breath. Then slowly exhale as you imagine the tension leaving your body. Repeat this four times, each time becoming more aware of your breathing.
- Let all your muscles relax as much as you can before going through the following steps.

- Tense the muscles of your feet and ankles, curling your toes. Gently release this tension until your feet and ankles are totally relaxed.
- Tense the muscles in the lower part of your legs. Slowly release this tension.
- Tense the muscles in your upper legs. As before, slowly release the tension from your legs. Your legs, ankles, and feet should now be fully relaxed and feel like they are hanging limply.
- Tense your hips and abdomen. As before, let this area of your body relax slowly.
- Tense your chest and back muscles. Slowly, gently relax these muscles.
- Direct your attention to your hands. Quickly make two fists, and slowly relax your hands.
- Bend your wrists. Then relax them.
- Tense the muscles in your lower arms. Slowly let them relax. Do the same with your upper arms.
- Shrug your shoulders. Let them relax. Shrug them a second time, and then let them relax even more. Your arms are now beginning to hang comfortably by your sides.
- Turn your head from side to side as far as it will go. Do this again. Touch your chin to your chest, and then raise it as high as you can. Relax your neck muscles.
- Clench your teeth tightly together. Now relax your jaw muscles. Smile as broadly as you can. Then relax your mouth. Wrinkle your nose. Relax it. Close your eyes tighter. Relax them. Wrinkle your forehead. Relax it, feeling the tension flow out of your head.
- If there still are any tense muscles in your body, direct your attention to these muscles. Relax them one-by-one.

Your body should now be totally relaxed. To ensure that your mind is also relaxed, visualize yourself in a quiet, peaceful setting. In Bobbie Stevens and Dean Portinga's course, they suggest visualizing a blue sky with one fluffy white cloud floating above you. You can relax your mind as you direct your attention to this fluffy white cloud. Now, visualize yourself floating high above the earth on this fluffy cloud in the blue sky. As you float on this cloud, let all of the stress and tension leave your mind. This has worked very well for me. Although it's been several years since I took Bobbie and Dean's course, I still think of them every time I see fluffy white clouds in the sky. I also still think of my first attempt at visualization and the wonderful results that I have created in my life from this process.

4. Create a mental movie.

Eleanor Roosevelt said, "The future belongs to those who believe in the beauty of their dreams." As human beings, not only can we dream, but also we can make our dreams come true. You are now ready to start creating your future through visualization and to put yourself on the path to realizing your vision.

At this point, bring one of the choices from your list into your mind. Picture yourself as if you have this in your life. The important word here is *picture*. Visualization works best in pictures, not paragraphs. In *Control Theory*, William Glasser says, "Most people do not know that they are motivated by the pictures in their heads and have no idea of how powerful and specific they are. . . . The power of pictures is total . . . and when we change the important pictures, we change our lives."

Dennis Deaton advises visualizing these pictures as sensory-rich, emotion-laden images. He says, "The more sensory-rich and emotion-laden the images, the more powerful they are to the subconscious, the more quickly they are absorbed, and the more readily they are acted upon."

Envision yourself using all of your senses in your mental movie.

- **Sight:** For my position in Europe, I could see the house and the car, as well as the autumn colors in the trees. Lois Crandell could see the Pacific Ocean. We both saw ourselves in decision-making settings where we had a major impact on the growth of our respective businesses.
- **Hearing:** I could hear people speaking English in different accents. Lois could hear the waves breaking on the shore.

- **Smell:** I could smell French perfume and Belgian waffles. Lois could smell the many fragrant flowers around her dream home by the ocean.
- **Taste:** I could taste the rich Belgian chocolates. Lois could taste the fresh seafood.
- **Touch:** In my vision, I could see myself holding onto a strap to support myself as I stepped onto a European train while traveling from one country to another. Lois could feel the wind on her face as she sailed on the ocean.

William Glasser said, "The way all creatures make contact [with the outside world] is through the senses associated with our eyes, ears, fingers, tongues and noses. But it is important to keep in mind that it is through these same senses that we make contact with our own minds and bodies."

While visualizing, let yourself also concentrate on how you feel emotionally and spiritually. If you are committed to your vision, these feelings will be good. When you have finished your visualization, slowly open your eyes.

5. Reinforce your vision through consistent mental rehearsal.

Your first visualization session might take some time; however, it is time well invested. Future visualization sessions might take anywhere from one to thirty minutes, depending on the circumstances. I recommend that you plan to visualize your goals and dreams at least twice each day and that you keep the end result in your thoughts throughout the day. Through your thoughts, you are creating your life. Your mind will then drive your actions in the direction of your dominant thoughts.

You have seen that visualization has worked in the lives of many successful people. You are probably now wondering how it works and how it differs from daydreaming. In *The Book on Mind Management*, Dr. Dennis Deaton states, "Vision is the element that integrates all of your faculties. When you visualize your goals in sensory-rich, emotion-laden images, you unite conscious mind, subconscious, and the energy and passions of the body into one unified force. The melding of all of your faculties vaults you to the highest attainable levels of human performance." He summarizes the process by the following four steps:

- The conscious mind activates the subconscious mind with the dominant thought.
- The subconscious mind develops plans to realize the dominant thought. It then flashes the plans to the conscious mind for evaluation.
- The conscious mind evaluates and approves the plans.
- The subconscious mind governs the body to bring the plans into working reality.

Other experts have made the following statements on the benefits of visualization:

"When we change the models in our mind, we change the results in our life." (Mark Victor Hansen, coauthor of *Chicken Soup for the Soul* series)

"Vividly experienced imagery, imagery which is both seen and felt, can substantially affect the brain waves, blood flow, heart rate, skin temperature, gastric secretions, and immune response . . . in fact the total physiology." (Jean Houston in *The Possible Human*)

"All thoughts which have been emotionalized [given feeling] and mixed with faith, begin immediately to translate themselves into their physical equivalent or counterpart." (Napoleon Hill in *Think and Grow Rich*)

"Your nervous system cannot tell the difference between an imagined experience and a 'real' experience. In either case, it reacts automatically to information which you give it from your forebrain." (Dr. Maxwell Maltz in *Psycho-Cybernetics*)

"Each time you 'see' yourself performing exactly the way you want with perfect form, you physically create neural patterns in your brain." (Kay Porter and Judy Foster in *The Mental Athlete*)

"As long as the mind can envision the fact that you can do something, you can do it. I visualized myself being there already—having achieved the goal already." (Arnold Schwarzenegger)

"We become what we think about all day long." (Ralph Waldo Emerson)

"It has been said that [the] picturing power of the mind is the greatest gift that God has ever given to man. It has the ability to construct images of success before the actual experiences are born. It can paint pictures that will fire our wills and exalt our spirits. This ability to travel ahead of our own success can draw us on with the greatest pleasure towards the most worthwhile objectives." (Sterling W. Sill in *The Upward Reach*)

— — —

In a dramatic manner, Dennis Deaton exposes his class participants to the Michelangelo Principle, which is "Masters *see* their creations *before* they are created." The Academia delle Arte houses one of the finest art collections in Europe. The most breathtaking sculpture in this museum is one of Michelangelo's best, the statue of David. This sculpture is not only massive, but it is also perfect in every detail. The visitor to the museum not only sees the muscle definition in the legs, but she also sees the veins and tendons in the hands, wrists, and feet. When he saw *David*, Dennis reminded himself that some human being had chipped, chiseled, and carved this figure out of dense, unrelenting marble.

As a result of his visit, Dennis decided to look into the history of the creation of *David*. He learned that, in 1501, the city-state of Florence commissioned Michelangelo to create a giant statue to be positioned in a prominent city square. There existed, at that time, a huge block of white marble that had been severely damaged and thought to be unfit for an average work of art, much less for a masterpiece. Michelangelo studied the block carefully, not only doing abstract mathematical calculations in his head, but also visualizing the end result of his creation. After visualizing *David*, he knew that this was the block he would use. He saw that the flaws did not cut through the figure in the stone. *David* lived so vividly in his mind that he saw his creation in the present tense before he ever even took the chisel into his hand to carve it.

Dr. Deaton's story of the statue, *David,* lived so vividly in my mind that I knew I also wanted to see this work of art. I added this to my visualization of my European job. Now, after 500 years, thousands of people are inspired each day by the vision and work of this great master. Many, such as I, are also inspired by the Michelangelo Principle and what it can do in our lives.

In the beginning of this chapter, I reviewed the visualization process that I used to create the experience of living and working in Europe. As I visualized this over the next several weeks, the vision became clearer. I made modifications in my vision as I clarified my goals and desires. The brown house in Belgium became a white stucco house with French shutters in the country outside of Paris, France. The red Audi was changed to a French-made automobile, a Renault top-of-the-line Safrane. I could still smell the Belgian waffles and knew that I wanted to spend at least one day each week in Brussels, attending meetings with Europeans and other Americans and visiting with my brother and sister-in-law who were living there.

In July of that year, I received a phone call from the vice president of 3M Europe. It was exactly as I had visualized it. In fact, I could have written the script for this conversation! He offered me the position and said that they were still trying to determine whether I would be headquartered in Paris or Brussels. In September, we found the perfect house, which had six bedrooms and thirteen bathrooms, in a scenic Paris suburb. We moved there in November, when I started my job as European marketing and sales productivity and quality manager. I had offices in both Paris and Brussels and traveled eighty percent of the time. Since our children were grown, my husband Cliff was able to travel with me much of the time. We saw magnificent beauty and history in fourteen European countries, both those included in my vision and others. While accomplishing my business and professional objectives, I made many new European friends and strengthened existing relationships.

One of my most memorable days in Europe was the day that I was able to see Michelangelo's *David* with my own eyes. He is just as magnificent as I had imagined him to be. Again I was reminded that masters see their creations before they are created. How true this had become for me! It will become true for you, also, if you believe in the power of your dreams and invest your energy in that direction.

CHAPTER

Determine Your Priorities!

Living them each day

Throughout much of my adult life, I considered myself one of the biggest victims of the Superwoman Syndrome. I completed two college degrees while working full time and raising two children. This might have been enough to undertake, but I didn't stop there. It was as if I wanted to show the world and myself that I could do it all—and do it perfectly. I made great meals and kept a spotless house. After finishing the dinner dishes and putting the children to bed each evening, I would scrub the kitchen floor (on my hands and knees) before doing my schoolwork. People would comment that my basement floor was so clean that they thought they could eat off of it. Weekends were my time to catch up with the things I was not able to accomplish during the week. I often felt guilty for not doing more.

One of the reasons that I was able to be so productive was that I made lists of the things that I needed to do. By following the lists, I didn't need to take the time to think about what to do next. I enumerated the tasks on paper as they came into my head, but I didn't spend much time prioritizing the lists. Since I thought that I had to get all of these things done, the priority didn't seem very important. I would normally start at the beginning of the list and work my way to the end. However, the lists were usually so long that I rarely got all the way to the end. The remaining items would just be transferred to the next list.

On a warm Friday evening in July 1984, I made a very long list of the things I wanted to accomplish that weekend. One of the items on my list was to call my grandmother. She was my only living grandparent, and I loved her dearly. She was of Italian descent and one of the best cooks I had ever known. She would often call me at work to tell me that she had made spaghetti sauce and meatballs and that I should stop by after work to take this meal home with me. When I was sick, she would call every day to see how I was feeling. She cared very deeply for each of her children and grandchildren. She gave of herself and expected nothing in return. As I thought of her on this particular Friday evening, I reminded myself that I hadn't talked with her in a while. On my list, I wrote, "Call Grandma." With all of the many things on my list, I never got to this item.

I had a late meeting on Monday night, so I added my item to call Grandma to my Tuesday night list. Grandma died suddenly of congestive heart failure on Tuesday. I had never made the phone call. After all of these years, I still often dream about making that call to my grandmother.

After my grandmother's death, I started thinking more about the importance of people in my life. I visited my parents more often and wrote notes to people who were important to me. I knew that I cared about people, and I wanted them to know that, too. However, as time went on, the demands of everyday life as I had known it in the past began to take their toll on me. Once again, I allowed myself to be a victim, a person who never seemed to have time for things that did not have worldly deadlines. It took another death, this time of a close friend, to jolt me to the realization of the critical importance of making a commitment to priorities in my life.

My friend's name was Cliff, and I had known him since before the days of office cubicles. We had worked together as systems analysts. His desk was behind mine, and we shared one telephone between us. When I first knew him, he was a confirmed bachelor, who partied with his buddies at night and complained about the water in the shower hurting in the morning. Then he met the love of his life—a bright, caring woman named Chris. Cliff and Chris were married and had two children, a girl and a boy. They were a perfect American family.

Cliff was an excellent systems analyst and set high standards for his own performance. He was also one of the most ethical people I have ever known. For these reasons, I enjoyed working with him. We often collaborated on projects, even after we moved to different departments within the company. We remained good friends throughout the years, and I most enjoyed when he would talk about his wife and children. I can still picture the smile on his face and the light in his eyes when he spoke of his family.

When Cliff was forty-one years old, he was diagnosed with terminal cancer. At first, he requested that he have no visitors. When he later came to terms with his prognosis, he and Chris invited friends to take turns visiting him on Fridays during lunchtime. It was decided that two of us would visit each Friday and that we would bring lunch for the family to eat as we spent time with him. Because of my hectic schedule, I postponed my visit to Cliff until three weeks after receiving the invitation.

On the day before my scheduled visit, I awoke from a dream very early in the morning. In my dream, I was visiting Cliff. I was dismayed, because I did not have the lunch with me. When I walked into Cliff's house, the light was so bright that I could hardly open my eyes. I learned later that morning that he had passed away at precisely the time of my dream. When I explained to Chris how sorry I was that I had not seen him before he died, she replied that she had heard of my dream from another friend and that she believed that Cliff had come to say good-bye to me.

It took the deaths of two people, who were close to me, to make me realize how important it is to set priorities in my life. I had often joked that I needed to live at least 1,000 years to accomplish everything I wanted to do in life. Now, I finally understood that I needed to decide what was important to me and to do these things during the limited amount of time available to me on this earth.

Because of the importance of the subject, much has been written and taught on time management, life management, and self-management. However, most women still feel the pressures of too much to do in too little time. There are many reasons for this, one of which is the need for better prioritization.

All eighteen successful women interviewed for this book are able to accomplish those things that are important to them in life. They each have established prioritization techniques to help them align their activities with their values. They are able to distinguish between what is important and what is urgent. They focus on the important activities, which deliver value. They fully comprehend what President Dwight Eisenhower meant when he said, "Most things which are urgent are not important, and most things which are important are not urgent."

Many of us complain about interruptions in the course of the day that rob us of time we had planned to spend on the things that are important to us; however, we allow these interruptions to have power over us. We might also say that we have our priorities straight and then demonstrate otherwise through our actions. For example, think about how we use "call waiting." A person could be involved in an important telephone discussion with a loved one, but when she hears the call waiting beep, she immediately puts the loved one on hold while she takes the call from the unknown caller. When I last did this, I reflected on the message that my action might have given to the first person. I also reexamined my values and asked myself if my activities were aligned with them. I reminded myself of a quotation from Goethe, who said, "Things which matter most must never be at the mercy of things which matter least."

In *The 7 Habits of Highly Effective People*, Stephen Covey discusses four generations of time management. The first generation is characterized by notes and checklists. Through the years, we women have learned that it is easier to write things down and to keep checklists than it is to try to remember everything that we think we have to do. Many of us also do this for our husbands or significant others, and we affectionately call these lists the "honey do" lists.

Calendars and appointment books characterize the second generation. This is an attempt to look ahead and to schedule the future. The advent of the day planner has helped to integrate the checklist with the appointment book. This second generation has added some contributions in the area of organization for many people.

The third generation adds the concepts of prioritization, of clarifying values, and of comparing the relative worth of activities based on their relationship to those values. We will spend more time on this later in this chapter.

Covey introduced a fourth generation, which recognizes that "time management" is really a misnomer. He says, "The challenge is not to manage time, but to manage ourselves." He explains that we spend time in one of four ways and that there are two factors that define an activity. Theses two factors are *urgent* and *important*.

Urgent items require immediate attention, such as a ringing telephone. Urgent matters are usually visible and popular with others. They are often pleasant, easy, and fun to do. However, they are not necessarily a priority and are most often unimportant.

Important items relate to results. If something is important, it contributes to one's mission, values, and/or high-priority goals. Important matters usually require a person to be proactive. If we don't have a clear idea of what is important in our lives, we will often react to the urgent matters and ignore or dismiss those which are important.

According to Covey's model, we spend our time in the following four ways:

1. Activities which are urgent and important, e.g., deadline-driven projects
2. Activities which are important but not urgent, e.g., relationship building, planning
3. Activities which are urgent but not important, e.g., interruptions
4. Activities which are not urgent and not important, e.g., trivia

If we are managing our priorities, the majority of our time will be spent on those activities that are important and not urgent.

Time Management Exercise

The following exercise will help you determine how you spend your time. For the next two days, keep a list of your activities in either fifteen-minute or thirty-minute segments, whichever works best for you. When you are interrupted, list the nature of the interruption along with the amount of time that it took. At the end of the second day, you will see how you have spent your time and the approximate amount of time you have spent on each activity.

When you have finished the time recording, prepare four sheets of paper by labeling the first "Urgent/Important," the second "Important/Not Urgent," the third "Urgent/Not Important," and the fourth "Not Urgent/Not Important." Now transfer your activities from your time recording, along with the time allocations for each, to the appropriate sheets of paper. When you have completed this, ask yourself the following questions:

- Are all the items on the first sheet (Urgent/Important) really important? If not, take time now to transfer these items to the appropriate sheets.
- Are all the items on the second sheet (Important/Not Urgent) really important? If not, take time now to transfer these items to the appropriate sheets.
- How much of my time am I spending on the activities that are really important to me?
- If I am not spending the majority of my time on the items that are important to me, what can I change in my life in order to do this? This might involve scheduling non-interruptible time

for important activities, learning to say no, delegating tasks to others, or just eliminating activities that are not that important to you.

— — —

Gayle Crowell is an amazing executive with a big job and an equally big heart. When I met her, she was the chief executive officer of RightPoint, Inc., a company specializing in helping other companies to better understand their customers. As chief executive officer, she led RightPoint from startup status to becoming a $700 million company in less than two years. She is also the mother of six children, a licensed pilot, and a former first grade and college teacher.

I first met Gayle in Chicago where she was speaking at an eCommerce conference. Not only is she one of the most knowledgeable speakers in her field, but she also has a speaking style which totally captivates an audience. As soon as she finished her speech, I made my way to the front of the room and asked her if she would be available to speak at a conference that I was hosting for over 1,000 marketers later in the year. Fortunately, she was available, and this gave me an opportunity to learn more about her.

Gayle and I did not talk with each other between the day we originally met and the day before my conference. She had trained her assistant very well to handle the logistical details concerning her speech at the conference and to ensure that I was comfortable with the arrangement. When I asked her assistant about Gayle's speaker fee, she quoted an amount, told me that the amount was negotiable if it was higher than my budget, and stated that Gayle would like me to contribute this entire speaking fee to a charity, which she named. This was the first time in my entire career that I had hired a speaker or a consultant, who wanted me to donate the money that they earned. Because of my curious nature, I later asked Gayle about this. She responded, "I want to give back in many ways. Since I have been running a startup company and my family is my top priority, I don't have a lot of time. What I do have is money. I really enjoy speaking and helping people to learn. Since I don't have a lot of time to volunteer for specific charities, I have decided that one way to do this is to donate my speaking fees to the charities that I want to impact. Since I don't need the extra money and don't have a way to create more time in a twenty-four-hour day, this is a way that I can contribute. For this chapter of my life, it is a good way to give back."

One of the reasons that Gayle is extremely successful is that she has set priorities in her life and examines her actions based on these priorities. She said, "Being successful is one of those things that encompasses all of your life. At the end of every day, I go through a ritual to reflect on the day and on my life to ensure that my priorities are in order. I feel good about what I have done that day and look for things that I could have done better. When I go to bed at night, I feel good about who I am as a person. Not every day is perfect, of course, but, in general, I'm very satisfied."

Gayle then added, "I set a very high priority on my family. It's not just my family, but people. My priorities include my extended family and many close friends. I have a very strong commitment to my six children in helping to shape their growth and in spending the appropriate amount of time with them. This often is a challenge when you're running a startup company. It's important to have a commitment. With that commitment, I find the execution is fairly easy, because I can then use my organizational skills and whatever else I need to get things in the proper perspective. This is a very strong thing for me. When I have interviewed for jobs during my career, I have always made it a point during the interview process to inform the interviewers that my family is a very high priority for me and that I'm not a person who would sacrifice that. This has worked well for me."

Gayle defines success in terms of feeling good about who we are and the choices we are making. She said, "I think it is important, especially for women, to feel good about a number of aspects of our lives, regardless of the choices we have made in the past. In the fast-paced world in which we live, we sort of get pulled into our career, because it's most pressing with people hammering at us to get things done. But I think it's important to step back and to know that there are many pieces of our lives. Each of us has many roles in life, which might include daughter, mother, partner, spouse, employee, leader, etc. We need to define the roles that are most important to us. I believe that we live our lives in chapters. In one chapter, a career may be more important; in another, time with children will be a higher priority." She added that, in order to become successful, a woman must define these roles and determine which are most important to her during the current "chapter." She can then set priorities for this chapter of her life.

Living our priorities in each chapter of our life is important to success. During a time when my friend Maggie's life was out of balance, her teenage daughter jokingly told me, "I can remember the day that I was born. I even remember all of the people who were in the delivery room. There was my dad, a doctor, and two nurses." Of course, I asked about her mom. "Oh, she was at the office!" she said. Of course, this was said within earshot of her mother. Although Maggie often said that her family was her top priority, her actions demonstrated differently. Her daughter's remark helped her to realize that her actions were not aligned with what she professed to be her priorities for this phase of her life. She immediately committed to aligning her actions with her priorities.

What are the things that are most important to you during the current chapter of your life? Many experts in the field of life management advise us to have a personal mission statement and to be able to state what we see as the overall purpose of our life. Your purpose might include spirituality, personal growth and development, relationships, career, contributions to society, possibly even self-actualization. It could be simple or complex. Several years ago, when asked to articulate my personal mission statement, without putting a lot of thought into it, I said that my mission was to help others to achieve their dreams. This is still one of my top priorities.

If you have not yet defined your purpose, I would suggest that you spend some time thinking about this during the next few days. It will then be easier to set priorities and to accomplish related tasks.

Whether or not you have clearly defined your personal mission statement, you can still determine your priorities. The following steps have worked for many successful women, and they will work for you.

1. Determine your true values.

If you were asked to develop a list of your values right now, would they be your honest values, or would they be a list of values you think you should have? Keep this question in mind as you engage in this exercise.

Start by making a list of items that you value most in life. Your value list might include some of the following:

- Relationship with spouse/significant other
- Relationship with children
- Relationship with other family members
- Spirituality
- Health and physical fitness
- Close friendships
- Rewarding and exciting career
- Financial independence
- Sports and recreation
- Personal development and growth
- Travel
- Community or church service
- Education
- Talent development
- Hobby and leisure activities

Your list will also include some of your personal values that are not listed above.

2. Prioritize your value list.

During this exercise, you will be working with your top seven values. If you have listed more than seven, you can use the following method to decrease the number to seven.

1. Determine whether any of your values have similar meanings. If so, combine them into one value statement.

2. If you have seven (or fewer) values on your list, go to number 10.

3. If you have more than fourteen values on your list, cross out the ones that are least important to you until you have just fourteen (or fewer) items remaining on the list.

4. Find the top value from your list, and put an asterisk in front of it.

5. Now find your lowest priority value, and cross it out.

6. If you now have just seven values on your list, go to number 10.

7. Find your next highest value. Put an asterisk in front of it.

8. From the remaining list, find the value that now has the lowest priority on the list. Cross it out.

9. If you still have more than seven values remaining on your list, go back to number 7. Otherwise, continue by going to number 10.

10. From this exercise, you should now have a list of your top values. If you so desire, you can prioritize these values using the same method. To do this, write the number "1" in front of your top value. Then write the number "7" in front of the lowest value on this list (if you have seven values listed). Next, write the number "2" in front of your highest of the remaining values on your list, write the number "6" in front of the lowest of the remaining values, and so forth. If you have fewer than seven values listed, you can make the necessary adjustments to these instructions. For many people, this process of selection and elimination works better than just trying to select first, second, and third priorities in sequence. The major result is that this will help you to determine which of the many activities on your daily "to do" list best fits within your value system and are, therefore, your highest priorities.

3. Plan and prioritize your activities.

Victor Hugo said, "He who every morning plans the transaction of the day and follows out that plan, carries a thread that will guide him through the maze of the most busy life. But where no plan is laid, where the disposal of time is surrendered merely to the chance of incidence, chaos will soon reign."

As Stephen Covey noted, most of us develop checklists. This is the first step toward prioritization of our activities. Although it is important to develop action lists for each day, some women prefer to work from a master list, which feeds their daily lists. Before I moved to Europe, I had the longest high-priority action list I have ever had. My colleagues teased me when I told them that I had put this list into an electronic spreadsheet and sorted it by the latest date that I could start each activity. But it worked!

The daily action list should include not only urgent activities, but also important activities that are not urgent. It should contain some time set aside for your values. For example, if one of your values is physical fitness, include a related activity on your action list at least three times per week. If your priority values include spiritual growth, you will want to reflect this on your action list.

You might have a big project that is important but not urgent. In many cases, you will not be able to complete this project in a day. It might require several days, weeks, or even months. In this case, you can divide this project into manageable segments and develop milestones for the segments. This offers several benefits:

- The project will not seem as overwhelming as it might have if you were to try to tackle it entirely at once.
- It is easier to concentrate on smaller tasks. The old saying that it is "easiest to eat an elephant one bite at a time" is true.
- By getting part of the project done on a daily basis, you are in a better position to complete the project on time.
- You are working on something that you classify as important.

It is best to prioritize a daily action list at the beginning of the day or at the end of the preceding day. There are many ways to prioritize the daily list. One way would be to compare the tasks with your values and to give highest priorities to those items which correspond with your highest values.

Another way to prioritize your daily action list would be to use the ABC method, where you would assign an "A" to the imperative tasks, a "B" to the other important tasks, and a "C" to all other tasks. Once you have done this, take another look at the items to which you have assigned a "C" priority. Are these the things that you really need or want to do? Is there someone else who could do them? This will be your decision. Once you have made this decision, you are ready to go ahead with your "A" priorities. When you have finished your "A" priorities, you are ready to start on your "B" priorities.

Many days, you will not complete all of the tasks on your action list. But, most days, you will complete your "A" priorities and some of your "B" priorities. You will then move the tasks, which have not been completed, to another day's list.

4. Make time for your highest priorities.

How often have you heard someone say, "I just do not have enough time?" The truth is that they have the exact same amount of time as you do, as I do, and as the successful women whom I interviewed for this book. The difference is in how they choose to spend or control their time and their tasks. To gain more control, it helps to ask ourselves, "Is this what I want or need to be doing right now?" If not, the prioritized action list will help to get back on track.

Learn to say no to requests and demands that do not fit into your priorities or help you to achieve your goals. In *101 Ways To Make Every Second Count*, Robert W. Bly says, "I had to learn to say no to requests, invitations, and offers that would neither make me happy nor help me to achieve my goals. But once I did it, I found that it was a liberating experience that gets easier with repetition."

Eliminate time-consuming activities that do not fit within your priority values. For me, scrubbing the kitchen floor every night was time-consuming. I value cleanliness, but this was carrying it to the extreme. I found that I could scrub the floor less often, and my kitchen was still clean enough. Later, when I became more successful in my career and my income grew, I hired a housecleaning service to do this for me. I discovered the secret of outsourcing those tasks that could be done by others and I could afford to pay others to do them. This freed some of my time to do the things that I enjoyed most and which contributed to my success.

One of my values is to give of myself to others. Many years ago, I took up the hobby of counted cross-stitching. I would spend hundreds of hours on one wall hanging and then give it to a friend or family member as a gift. A friend once asked how much time I had spent on a particular gift. She then calculated how much money this gift was worth by multiplying the number of hours by the hourly rate I would have made if I had been working at my occupation during the hours that I spent creating this gift. The amount was staggering; however, the gift was priceless to the receiver, I had engaged in an activity that I enjoyed, and the creation of this gift was within my value priorities. By freeing up my time in other ways, I was able to spend more time on this priority activity.

Another way to free up your time is to delegate as much as possible. Many of us women are perfectionists, who think that we are the only ones who can perform a particular task or that we can do it better than anyone else can. This reminds me of the song about "anything you can do, I can do better." With this attitude, we can spend too much time on tasks that do not contribute to our success.

In *How Men Think: The Seven Essential Rules for Making It in a Man's World*, Adrienne Mendell, M.A., says the following about delegation:

> The ability to delegate work is an essential skill. Skillful delegating takes time and assertiveness. It increases your productivity, but it does have some drawbacks. When you delegate, you give up some control of the work, and you might have to accept work that is adequate but not as good as yours would have been.
>
> But you lose much more by not delegating. If you don't delegate, it takes longer to finish projects. You risk becoming mired in routine work and not having time

for new, challenging assignments. You won't have time to learn new skills or be creative. If you don't have time to volunteer for assignments to display your skills, you hurt your chances of advancement. In most companies, ability to delegate is one of the criteria used to evaluate managers.

Delegation works, not only in the business environment, but also in the home and in other organizations. It is not necessary to have employees reporting to us in order to delegate. Those of us who are mothers have delegated to our children. In the corporate world, I have delegated both to those who report to me and to my boss, when I knew that he would enjoy the task I was requesting that he handle.

My delegation-style varies depending on the person to whom I am delegating. In the corporate world, I have been fortunate in that I have been able to select and hire highly motivated, enthusiastic and committed people. This makes delegation easy. However, most executives and managers also inherit people when we move into new positions, and we need to be able to delegate effectively to those whom we may not have selected in the first place.

Following are some of the rules that I have set for myself and followed in delegating to employees:

- Have confidence in the employee, and expect that he or she will do the task well.
- Treat the employee as I want others to treat me. Show the employee that I know that he or she will do the task well.
- As much as possible, match the project with the employee's skills and desires. Also, if possible, allow some leeway that will help the employee grow and develop in the job.
- Delegate the authority to accomplish a task along with the responsibility.
- Don't delegate projects or tasks that are impossible for the employee to do. Eliminate roadblocks along the way.
- Explain the assignment clearly. Ensure that the employee knows what is expected as far as results and timing.

- After delegating a project or task, get out of the employee's way. Make sure that the employee knows what is expected. Be available if he or she has questions or needs assistance.
- For longer projects, ask for periodic status reports. Make it clear that the supervisor needs to be kept in the loop.
- Give the employees credit for the work that they do. Match the recognition with the project and the employee.

This list of "rules" also works when delegating to children or anyone else.

To create success in our lives, we need to define and prioritize our values and to live by the priorities we set for ourselves.

After having held senior management positions at Citicorp/ Citibank, Xerox, and Bell Atlantic, Laraine Rodgers founded her own consulting company. Her company, which was based in Phoenix, Arizona, provided vision and leadership to help organizations effectively link technology with business and people in order to achieve their customer, value, and revenue goals. She enjoyed consulting, and this was very lucrative financially.

Laraine says her top priorities are to enjoy each day and to continue learning. Although she enjoyed success in the consulting business, she discovered that the amount of necessary travel conflicted with achieving her priorities. She thought about this when a large company recently pursued her for a top management position. She was interested in the position, but she had learned from her consulting business that she was not willing to compromise her priorities. When she interviewed for the position, she told the interviewers that she absolutely would not travel more than four nights per month. She said, "If you offer me this position and want me to travel more than that, I guess that means that you're firing me, and that's okay with me." She was offered the position and accepted it. Although she enjoyed her consulting business, her new position offers her the opportunity to live within her priorities more so than any other position she has held in the past.

Laraine later told me, "There's a part of me that was so afraid inside, maybe my whole life, to say no and then take the consequences, whatever they might be. This was a milestone that I achieved this year. This was a success. I'm really glad that I pushed back, and now I'm doing exactly what I want with this company."

Betty Notto is a remarkable woman. She is a much-loved wife, mother, grandmother, great-grandmother, and friend. She says that her top priority is her family, and she lives this priority. One Saturday, after a typically busy week, she was looking forward to spending the day at home cleaning her house and taking some time for relaxation. The phone rang shortly after she finished breakfast. It was her twelve-year-old granddaughter, Kayla.

"What are you doing today, Grandma?"

"Oh, I'm just planning to clean the house. I've been involved with my volunteer activities all week, and the house looks like I have neglected it. What are you doing?"

"Nothing. My friend and I wanted to go shopping at the mall, but our parents are busy and can't take us."

"Do you want me to pick you up at your house and drop you off at the mall? I can go back to the mall later to get you and take you home."

"No, my parents won't allow me to go to the mall without an adult."

At this point, Betty volunteered to go shopping with Kayla and her friend. She spent the day in the stores where young girls like to shop. She later told me that she heard more rock music that day than she had in the past twenty years. Her house was not as clean as she had planned, but she had done something that she considered much more important. Kayla enjoyed the day with her friend and her grandmother. As she gets older, she will realize even more how much she treasures the time her grandmother spends with her. She will also understand how her grandmother has set priorities and has lived within those priorities. If she follows the example set by her grandmother, she will be on the path to success.

By using the methods specified in this chapter, we are able to make time to do those things that are most important to us. When our values are prioritized before writing a "to do" list, we are better able to determine when an *urgent* item is an *important* item and act accordingly.

CHAPTER

Set Powerful Goals!

Expanding your horizons

My office dictionary defines the word *goal* as "the purpose toward which effort is directed." We are all engaged in some type of effort each day, but are we all working toward a known purpose? If you have read *Through the Looking Glass*, you might remember the quote, "If you don't know where you're going, any road will get you there." To be successful, it is important to know where it is that you want to go.

Do you know where you are going? Do you know the purpose toward which your efforts are directed? Successful people set goals and direct their efforts toward achieving them. However, fewer than five percent of all people have goals. In the course of my career, I have heard the following excuses for not setting goals:

- *"I am a busy person. I don't have time to think about setting goals."* I hope this person reads Chapter 3 of this book on setting priorities around her values.
- *"It doesn't pay for me to set goals, because I keep changing my mind about what I want."* One of the steps in the goal-setting process is to clarify wants and needs.

- *"I set a goal once and didn't achieve it."* I question whether this person was committed to the goal and whether she had developed an action plan for achieving the goal. There will be more on this later.

The first step to achieving a goal is to have a goal. Nancy Albertini is founder and chief executive officer of Taylor Winfield, a Dallas-based executive search firm specializing in placing CEOs and other executives in the high-technology market. Before founding this company, she set a goal to affect people's lives in a positive way. As a result, she created Taylor Winfield, a company that enriches the lives of its employees, the people they place, and the people who do the hiring. Nancy also set a financial goal for her company. Not only has the company achieved that goal, but they have more than quadrupled it.

When she was very young, Wendy Richards had a goal to live overseas. She thought about this goal while she was in high school and, when the time came, chose to attend a university that offered the possibility of an overseas experience. She decided that she wanted to live in Germany and began to study the German language, as well as the languages of neighboring countries. She met this goal and studied for a year in Berlin, while living with a German family.

After her year in Germany, Wendy returned to the United States and vigorously enhanced her goal to include working in Europe during her career. She completed her bachelor of arts degree in history at Stanford University, where she received Phi Beta Kappa honors and graduated with distinction. She then proceeded into the MBA program at Stanford University. She graduated as the Arjay Miller Scholar, in the top ten percent of her Stanford MBA class.

Wendy's education prepared her well for international employment. After finishing her MBA, her first position was as an international market development manager for Activision, where she used many of the strategies in this book to establish and manage European subsidiaries in England, France, and Germany and structured licensing agreements for Japan. In her early thirties, she became the director of international strategic planning for a large telecommunications company. She was later transferred to Brussels, Belgium, to serve as the managing director for that company in Belgium. Her career has progressed from that point to include top management positions in large international companies, where she has had the opportunity to live and work in several European countries.

Wendy set her goals while she was still very young, and she has accomplished every goal that she has set for herself. Not all of us start this process as young as this. Many of us, including several of the successful women that I have interviewed, have taken gigantic detours along the way. This is especially true of me. However, at some point, we have all learned the value of setting powerful goals and have been able to achieve tremendous success as a result.

Before setting goals, it is important to become extremely clear in determining what it is that we really want. In Chapter 2, we discussed the visualization process, and you did some work in determining your wants and desires. Now that you have completed Chapter 3 and determined your values and related priorities, it is time to revisit your list of choices you used in the visualization process. Are these choices congruent with your values and priorities in life? If not, now is the time to make some adjustments.

When I first determined that I wanted to live and work in Europe, I wasn't totally clear on where I wanted to live on the European continent. During my first visualization exercise, I pictured myself living in Brussels, Belgium. I later realized that this was because Brussels was the location of my company's European headquarters, and I thought that I had to live in Brussels in order to do the type of work that I wanted to do. As I clarified my goal, I realized that I really wanted to live near Paris, France, and still have the opportunity to spend as much of my business time as possible in Brussels. The clarification gave me the best of both worlds—a home in France and offices in both France and Belgium.

I truly believe that each of us is the chief executive officer of our own life. In order for a woman to be successful as a CEO, she needs to take charge of her life. She needs to realize that she creates the life she wants. Before doing this, she needs to know who she is and what she wants. She needs to seek clarity in doing this and in setting goals for her life.

In Bobbie Stevens' course and also in her book, *Unlimited Futures: How to Understand the Life You Have and Create the Life You Want*, she teaches what she calls "Seven Steps of the Creative Process." Visualization is one of these steps. Seeking clarity is another one. An earlier example in this book shows that Bobbie was very clear that she wanted to buy a town house, even though town houses did not exist where she lived and she did not earn enough money at the time. With her clear goal and vision, however, she was able to create the steps necessary to accomplish this. She lists seeking clarity as the first step in creating what one wants in life.

Those who recognize the value of setting powerful goals are the people who create success. Many of these people are now enjoying success they would not have imagined had they not taken the time to set these goals. Goal setting is simple, once you have clarified your wants and desires. The following tips will help you to set and achieve powerful goals for yourself.

1. Write them down.

I once listened to a tape series where the speaker encouraged listeners to write on a piece of paper the amount of money they wanted to be making a year from then. He then said to seal the paper in an envelope and to wait one year to open the envelope. I wanted to be making much more money than I was earning at the time, but I worked for a corporation that had a set salary scale and ranges of percentages for salary increases. Nevertheless, I wrote down a number that was $30,000 more than I thought possible if I continued to work for this company. Although I did not change companies, I was thrilled one year later when I opened the envelope and discovered that my new salary was exactly what I had written. The contributing factors were that I had a goal, this goal was written, and I changed my work patterns to accomplish it. I also believe that, once a goal is written or "put out into the Universe" in another way, there are other factors that work with us in accomplishing this goal. For example, during this time, salary scales were changed, I received two promotions, and profit sharing for my company was at an all-time high. I had not considered these factors when I decided how much money I would like to be earning.

Fewer than five percent of all people have goals, and three percent have written goals. Since these are the people who most often achieve their goals, they have a difficult time understanding why the other ninety-seven percent don't write their goals. Nancy Albertini also suggests that it is important to state a goal out loud both to ourselves and to others. She once went with a friend to a visualization session on success. Most of the women in attendance were talking about small, incremental steps that they would like to make in their lives. Nancy announced that her goal was to quadruple her net worth by the time she was fifty. The other attendees looked at her in astonishment. If her net worth was $100 or even $100,000, this goal might not have been as amazing; however, her net worth already was considerable. Nancy not only met this goal, but she also quadrupled it again and she still has several more years before her fiftieth birthday.

A goal becomes much more powerful when it is written down. Alexander Graham Bell observed, "What this power is I cannot say; all I know is that it exists, and it becomes available only when a [woman] is in the state of mind in which [she] knows exactly what [she] wants and is fully determined not to quit until [she] finds it."

2. Ensure that your goals are realistic and achievable, but give them some "stretch" to allow room for growth.

Nancy Albertini's financial goal certainly had stretch. My financial goal also had stretch, although of a lesser magnitude than Nancy's. This is important in goal setting. Most of us don't realize the power within us to achieve greatness. The French spiritual philosopher, Teilhard de Chardin, said, "It is our duty to proceed as if limits to our ability do not exist." Successful women always set higher goals.

Are your goals big enough? Are they worthy of you? You were born with unlimited capacity in many areas. In these areas, you are limited only by your own beliefs.

Terri Bowersock was born with dyslexia, a learning disability. She struggled through school and vividly recalls that one of her teachers hit her on the head with a ruler and said she was "as dumb as a cue ball." Terri herself could easily have believed she was stupid and incapable of accomplishing anything of value. She also could have believed that she would not be able to achieve any goals if she were to set them for herself; however, she was determined to succeed. She was able to graduate from high school, even though she could read only at a third-grade level. In her early twenties, she set a goal to become successful in the furniture consignment business, which was a business that hardly existed at that time. She started by borrowing $2,000 from her grandmother and opened a shop. Her first sales were her mother's living room furniture and her own bedroom set. She progressed from there, setting and achieving powerful goals along the way. Twenty-one years later, she now owns and manages five companies. She has sixteen consignment furniture stores nationwide and continues to expand her enterprises. Her annual sales exceed $26 million, and she is a sought-after motivational speaker. She has been named "Entrepreneurial Woman of the Year" by *Entrepreneur Magazine* and has won the *Inc. Magazine* "Retail Entrepreneur of the Year" award. When she was featured on the *Oprah Winfrey Show*, Oprah said, "Terri knows the secrets to realize her dreams." This all started when Terri set her first goal to open a furniture consignment store.

Many of us have physical limitations that must be taken into consideration when we set our goals. However, in case after case, I have seen women circumvent these physical limitations and set and achieve goals that strengthen them. Some may need to think about setting powerful goals in alternate areas of their lives where they are not affected by the physical limitation. Regardless, we can all set powerful goals and achieve them.

3. Clearly define your goals.

As you write a goal, it is important to give a clear definition of the results you are planning. Check to ensure that it answers the following "W" questions:

- Who? (In most cases, this will be ourself.)
- What? (We need to describe the end result of our goal.)
- Where? (This has to do with location. If it is a job-oriented goal, it might be the company or department where we will achieve the results.)
- When? (Include the date on which the goal will be accomplished. If it is a long-term goal, it is also good to include some milestone dates.)

Once you are sure that the goal answers the "W" questions, check the goal to make sure that it is measurable. Ask yourself, "How will I know that I have achieved this goal?"

———

Born in rural Arkansas, Kathy Brittain White was the daughter of a construction worker and a high school home economics teacher. She didn't think much about goals when she graduated from high school, but she thought that she wanted to finish college and follow in her mother's footsteps as a home economics teacher. As an eighteen-year-old college freshman, she married a serviceman who was transferred from base to base. She would go with him and take some college courses wherever they were living. Since she had taken secretarial courses, she was secure in the thought that she could always find a good office job wherever they lived. When she and her husband returned to Arkansas, she was pregnant with her second child. "We were broke and living in a horrible place," she told me. One day, she said she experienced a defining moment. "This is the way it is always going to be if I don't make it different," she realized. She then set a powerful educational goal for herself. She started university correspondence courses during her pregnancy and completed her undergraduate degree in a year. "I kept going to school," she said. "I just went on. I got an assistantship at Arkansas State

University where I was going to school. I never stopped until I finished my doctorate."

Kathy continued to set powerful goals for herself. The year she completed her doctorate degree, she became an associate professor at the University of North Carolina, conducting primary and secondary research on information technology best practices, systems implementation success, and metrics. She wrote more than thirty articles that were published in major publications and spoke frequently at national and international conferences.

Kathy continued on her goal-oriented path. Her next goal was to become an executive in the corporate world. She moved from the education world to the corporate world as the vice president of a major corporation. She is now executive vice president and chief information officer of Cardinal Health, Inc., a major healthcare company. Her worldwide staff totals more than 1,500 people. She continues to clearly define her goals, which include family, relationships, career, and making a significant contribution in the world.

4. Visualize your goals as if you have already achieved them.

How do you feel about your goals? Do they excite you? Do they provide emotional energy? Do you dream about them at night? Do they get you up in the morning with a feeling of vigor for doing what needs to be done in order to achieve them? If not, you need to reevaluate your goals, values, and priorities.

Once you have clearly defined goals that excite you and to which you are committed, revisit Chapter 2 and repeat the visualization process for these goals. You originally engaged in this process to visualize what you thought you wanted the first time you read Chapter 2. Now you can become even more clear in your visualization. Henry David Thoreau stated it quite succinctly when he said, "If you have built castles in the air, your work need not be lost; that is where they should be. Now put the foundations under them." You can do this by setting, being committed to, continuing to visualize, and taking action on your goals.

For many women, concrete images of the results of these goals are also helpful. You might want to cut pictures from magazines or catalogues that will remind you of your goals. For example, if your goal is to live in your dream home, you can find or draw a picture of this house and put it in a place where you will see it often (your refrigerator, your bathroom mirror, your office, etc.). A friend who wants to get down to her high school graduation dress size has taped a picture of herself at this size to her refrigerator. A person who wants to live in Paris might do the same with pictures of the Eiffel Tower, Notre Dame Cathedral, and the Arc de Triomphe. These concrete, easily recognizable pictures will help you in the visualization process.

Goal setting significantly increases our opportunity for success. It is my belief that combining visualization with goal setting exponentially increases the successful outcome. In *The Law of Success*, Napoleon Hill said, "Any definite chief aim that is deliberately fixed in the mind and held there, with the determination to realize it, finally saturates the entire subconscious mind until it automatically influences the physical action of the body toward the attainment of that purpose."

Successful women recommend that we visualize our goals by using the process in Chapter 2 at least twice each day. The results that can be achieved by running these mental movies are much, much greater than the amount of time it takes to do this. Each of us is capable of greatness. Visualization will give the information to the subconscious mind, enabling it to help us in achieving our highest aspirations.

The Eastern sage and philosopher, Patanjali, once said, "When you are inspired by some great purpose, some extraordinary project, all your thoughts break their bounds. Your mind transcends limitations, your consciousness expands in every direction. . . . Dominant forces, faculties and talents become alive, and you discover yourself to be a greater person by far than you ever dreamed yourself to be."

5. Describe the benefits of your goals.

According to Dennis Deaton, a goal becomes more powerful when its benefits are expressed in the form of two specific statements:

• Personal, or self-directed, benefits
• Altruistic, or spiritual, benefits

Dr. Deaton recommends the development of a "Power Goal Manuscript," which includes the statement of the goal (including who, what, where, and when), a benefit statement, and a commitment statement.

When I first wrote my goal for living and working in Europe, I included the following benefit statement, which you read in Chapter 2:

> I am excited about this excellent opportunity to not only increase the company's sales and marketing effectiveness in Europe and enhance my career, but also to see and experience much of Europe, including the Vatican and the Leaning Tower of Pisa in Italy, the Eiffel Tower and the Louvre in Paris, the theater in London, the green rolling landscape of Ireland, the Alps, ancient cathedrals and museums.

> My husband Cliff and I look forward to making new acquaintances with many Europeans whom we expect to meet in the next two years. We are also eager to host many of our American friends and relatives while we are in Europe.

I later added the following to this benefit statement:

> As we look at the house, I think about how this will be my home base as I travel to seventeen different countries in Europe in developing a sales and marketing productivity plan. What an opportunity this is to contribute to the company's growth! By increasing sales and marketing productivity in Europe, 3M's sales in Europe will grow by at least five percent. I am excited about the opportunity to contribute to driving this growth.

I am also looking forward to becoming active in my church in Europe, to being a leader in the church women's organization, and to touching the hearts of many women through the education program.

Reviewing these benefits every day helped me to visualize and achieve my goal. Your benefit statement can be in paragraph form, or it can be a list. Whichever you choose, you'll want to be sure you can picture the benefits you describe. The pictures will then translate best to your subconscious mind as you engage in the visualization process.

6. Commit to accomplishing your goals.

When I wrote my goal for living and working in Europe, I included the following commitment statement:

I commit myself totally to this goal. I commit myself to continuing to learn about productivity through reading, videotapes, audiotapes, and seminars. I see myself working with others who specialize in this field. I see Cliff and me working to prepare for this move.

I commit myself to networking with those in the company who can assist in making this happen. This will include area vice presidents, managing directors, and human resource personnel.

I commit myself to developing a plan for building a sales and marketing productivity architecture for Europe. I will put my best effort into developing and implementing this plan.

If we are not willing to do what is needed to accomplish a goal, we may as well not even have a goal. A person might say that their goal is to be a millionaire. When asked what they are going to do to become a millionaire, they have no answer. Their goal is not a goal at all, but a fantasy. Goals require commitment and action.

7. Develop and implement an action plan.

As you engage in the visualization process, you picture yourself as if you have already achieved your goal. Your subconscious mind will help you to develop the process to get there, if you are in tune with and listen to its promptings. Women typically are successful in this process; that's where "women's intuition" comes into play. As you receive these promptings, pay attention to them. Then write them down.

Even early American leaders took intuitive thoughts seriously. Thomas Paine once said, "Any person who has made observations on the state of progress of the human mind cannot but have observed that there are two distinct classes of what are called thoughts: Those that we produce by ourselves by reflection and the act of thinking, and those that bolt into the mind on their own accord. I have always made it a rule to treat these voluntary visitors with civility, taking care to examine, as well as I was able, if they were worth entertaining; and it is from them I have acquired almost all the knowledge I have."

Italian artist Leonardo da Vinci stated, "The ideas that would suddenly come to my awareness proved to be most worthy and were in the end found to be infallible in leading me to discoveries of great importance."

These thoughts that bolt into our minds are often golden in nature. They have the potential to both solve problems and open doors of opportunity. They usually come during our most quiet times, as those are the times that we are most open to listening to them. I often receive these inspirational messages in the shower, as I am relaxing under the hot water. Others will receive these messages in the middle of the night during one of their lighter sleep cycles. It is advisable to have a tape recorder or paper and pen nearby in order to record these messages. These thoughts can also come during or immediately following a visualization session, prayer, or meditation. During these times, you may want to remain in your position for a few moments in order to receive these messages, and then write them down. Revisit your notes soon afterward to sort them out in your mind while they are still fresh.

As you start to develop your action plan for a major goal, you might want to engage in a brainstorming process with yourself. Start by writing your goal at the top of a piece of paper. During the next twenty minutes, write at least twenty things that you can do to accomplish this goal. As you are writing, do not ponder whether these things are possible; just keep writing. When you think you have thought of everything you can do to accomplish the goal, write five more things. The first five things you write will be obvious and probably will be things that anyone would have written. The more you write, the more your subconscious mind will deliver. The best ideas often will come after you have written sixteen or seventeen items.

You are now ready to develop your action plan for accomplishing your goal. If your goal is a long-term one, it will work best to divide it into shorter-term action plans, each for approximately ninety-day periods. After each three-month period, you can then evaluate and make adjustments in the plans for future segments. On the surface, large goals can seem intimidating. However, even ninety-day goals can be divided into a series of smaller action steps that are easy to plan, easy to integrate into daily activities, and fairly easy to accomplish. By doing this, we can accomplish even long-term, strategic goals without becoming overwhelmed.

In addition to listing the steps you will take to accomplish your goal, you might want to include the following in your plan:

- Resources needed
- Possible obstacles and alternative ways to work around these obstacles
- Support structure currently in place
- Type of support you will need in order to accomplish the goal
- Interim rewards for accomplishing action steps

In his tape series, *Peak Performance Woman*, Brian Tracy gives the following tips for goal achievement:

- Identify major obstacles to goal achievement. Ask yourself what stands between you and your goal. Some examples could be a relationship, health concerns, education, your boss, etc.
- Set a deadline and a schedule for accomplishment.

- Set a schedule for rewarding yourself as you reach milestones on the way to accomplishing your goal.
- Review your goals every morning and every evening.
- Be clear about what you want to accomplish, but be flexible in between.

He also recommends that you keep your mind on your previous successes.

As you have been reading this chapter, I hope you have taken the time to write your major goals and to ensure that they are aligned with your values and priorities in life. If you do not have written goals, I encourage you to write them now. If you want to create success in your life, this will be well worth the investment in time.

Dream big, and set powerful goals around these dreams. Ask yourself what goal you would set for yourself if you knew you would successfully achieve it. Next, ask yourself if this is what you really want. If it is, write it down. Then you can use what you have learned in this chapter to put yourself on the path to achieving this goal. A speaker at a conference I attended recently said, "Goals are the fuel in the furnace of achievement."

CHAPTER

Ready—Aim—Take Action!

Starting NOW

Abraham Lincoln said, "Things may come to those who wait, but only the things left by those who hustle." We build a foundation by visualizing what we want, determining our priorities, and setting goals. Once this is done, it is necessary to move forward by *taking action.* Standing still is the fastest way of moving backwards in this rapidly changing world.

As you engage in the visualization process, your subconscious mind will help you to develop an action plan to meet your goals. Sigmund Freud once declared, "Thought is action in rehearsal." Many successful athletes, as well as many business people, have put this concept into practice. One example is Jack Nicklaus, one of the most successful professional golfers of all time, who said, "I never hit a shot, not even in practice, without having a very sharp, in-focus picture of it in my head. It's like a color movie. First I 'see' the ball where I want it to finish, nice and white sitting up high on the bright green grass. Then the scene quickly changes, and I 'see' the ball going there: its path, trajectory and shape, even its behavior on the landing. Then there is a fade-out, and the next scene shows

97

me making the kind of swing that will turn the previous images into reality."

Jack Nicklaus uses visualization to create his success; however, he doesn't stop there. Immediately after visualizing the success, he takes action to ensure this success. Taking action differentiates those who only dream from those who have dreams and create success in their lives.

In physical stature, Charleen Tajiri is one of the most petite women I have ever met. When she first entered our meeting, I wondered if she bought her clothes in the children's department! Within minutes after she began her presentation, I had forgotten about her physical size. I was much more impressed with her dynamism, professionalism, and confidence. She is a successful businesswoman, who knows where she's headed and acts quickly to achieve her goals.

The first of six children born into a Hawaiian family, Charleen was raised for many of her childhood years by a single mother in a home with few, if any, luxuries. She attended the University of Hawaii and was the only one in her family to go to college. However, it wasn't until she was twenty-seven years old that she started to take charge of her life. Almost immediately, she became successful.

She did some volunteer work at a personal growth and development company. The company hired her as an employee a year later. She rose to the top of the company by working hard and developing strong management and leadership skills. Although her home was, and still is, in Honolulu, her reputation as a leader spread across the United States. As a result, a much larger seminar company on the mainland approached her and asked her to work for them from her Hawaii home office. She accepted the position and, within the first year, doubled the attendance at this company's seminars.

While holding leadership positions in the development and seminar companies, Charleen was also involved as a distributor for multiple companies, which sold their products through multilevel marketing channels. She quickly became a top distributor for each one of these companies. She currently owns and manages a company, which distributes nutritional products. With four partners, she also owns and manages a wholesale distribution company, which distributes a line of spices, novelty items, and snacks, nationwide.

Charleen believes in running a principle-centered business. Her family is her top priority. Her office is in her home, and this helps her to spend more time with her son. Her home is always open to family and friends. She is results-driven and takes the appropriate action to achieve successful results. She says, "It's when I take action that things really happen, even those things that I may not have thought about during the planning stage. More options and solutions seem to pop up as I'm working to achieve a goal."

Charleen agrees with Thomas Edison's statement, "Genius is one percent inspiration and ninety-nine percent perspiration." For her, the inspiration is the necessary foundation, but the action actually accomplishes the goal.

— — —

When Linda Herold moved to Scottsdale, Arizona, her primary goals were to establish herself in the community, develop relationships, and build a center of influence. She soon became a board member for the Arizona Small Business Association and received its Networking Excellence Award. She has since received awards for Distinguished Board Service and Outstanding Community Service. In addition, she was named the Small Business Journalist of the Year by the U.S. Small Business Administration—Arizona for 2000. She also chaired the Entrepreneurial Roundtable of the Arizona Small Business Association and was one of three distinguished honorees at the Impact for Enterprising Women's Annual "Celebration of Success."

Linda accomplished her goal in a very short time because she took immediate action. She started by publishing a newsletter for women in the Phoenix area. Each issue profiles thirty women, giving information on who they are, what they do, and how to connect with them. Her newsletter also gives information about events, organizations, and opportunities. She publishes an annual directory and sponsors a "meet the subscribers" party. In order to meet more women in her area, she cofounded a social organization called "Women of Scottsdale," which meets monthly for lunch. Because she is so active in the community, she is asked to chair many community events. She has developed the relationships she had originally sought and has made some close friends in her community.

Taking action was paramount to achieving her goal. "When I feel like procrastinating," she said, "I force myself to do something. I may not do it all at once, but, if I start, then I'm on the path. If I do part of it, even if it's just filling out one form or making an initial phone call, I'm committed."

— — —

Terry Swack, vice president of experience design for Razorfish, a global digital services provider, is another results-driven and action-oriented woman. When I first met her, she was CEO of TSDesign, a Boston-based Internet strategy and product design firm, which she had founded and managed for fourteen years. When use of the Internet started to grow in the mid-1990s, Terry expanded her company's services and began to specialize in Internet design. We hired TSDesign to audit our large corporate Internet site, and Terry herself took responsibility for managing the project. Based on the audit report, we decided to hire TSDesign to redesign the site.

About forty people attended our first meeting to discuss the Internet redesign. With that many attendees, an all-day meeting can be an information-only meeting. However, in conducting the meeting, Terry made sure that we formed teams to address the major issues. She gave specific instructions and assignments to each team and scheduled a follow-up meeting date to report on progress and to decide on next steps. Because of Terry's leadership, each of the forty people left the meeting with a well-defined action plan.

The group of people, who were involved in this project, soon grew from the original forty to more than 100 worldwide. Although the group consisted of committed top performers, it seemed that all of them had separate agendas in order to fit their individual business needs. Under Terry's coaching, they became a cohesive team working toward common goals for the company. She led them in the development and implementation of an action plan that met the company's goals and delivered results much faster than anyone would have thought possible before starting this project.

Terry's leadership of this project was typical of the way she does business. When she decided to sell her business, she looked for a company that had the same standards and mode of operation as her company. "The reason that Razorfish and I selected each other was that we both have a core belief that design makes a better world for people," she said. Once she was able to determine this, she made a decision and acted on that decision. Regarding the importance of taking action to her success, she said, "The ability to execute is what differentiates."

All of the successful women interviewed agreed that action is a predecessor to success. One woman said, "Just do it!" Another said, "If you don't act, nothing will happen." A third quoted Will Rogers, who stated, "Even if you're on the right track, you'll get run over if you just sit there."

Often the most difficult part of taking action is getting started. The best way to start is to first develop an action plan. Writing an action plan requires the action of writing. Your action plan can be simple or complex, depending on the nature of your goal. Following are examples of some simple action plans:

1. Jane's goal is to decrease her clothing size from fourteen to ten. Her action plan might include these steps:
   - Visualize myself as wearing a size ten.
   - Tape pictures to the refrigerator and bathroom mirror of myself from four years ago, when I wore a size ten.
   - Consult my doctor concerning the diet that is best for me.
   - Prepare weekly menu plans.
   - Make grocery lists before shopping for groceries.

- Shop for groceries after meals, and buy only those foods on the list.
- Eat only foods that are on my diet plan.
- Walk at least twenty minutes each day.
- Weigh and measure myself weekly.
- Reward myself with a visit to an art museum, a movie, or taking time to read a new book as I reach each five-pound milestone.

2. Eva's goal is to buy a new house. She might engage in the following action plan:

- Save money for a down payment on the new house.
- Study information about local communities and determine where I want to live.
- Visualize my new home.
- List the features that I want in my new home.
- Interview real estate agents, and select the one who will work best with me.
- With the selected real estate agent, tour homes that are in my selected area, which have the features I want and are within my price range.
- Revisit the homes that best match my selection criteria.
- Make an offer to purchase the house.
- Celebrate, and move in!

3. Marcia is twenty-six years old. She is married, has two small children, and works full-time. She has completed two years of college. Her goal is to complete her bachelor's degree by her thirtieth birthday. This is a longer-term goal and will probably require some decision analysis, as well as short-term action steps. Her action plan to enroll in a degree program might consist of the following steps:

- Visualize myself at a college commencement walking to the stage in cap and gown to receive my diploma.
- Determine the major area of study that best fits what I want to do in the future.
- Determine how I will finance my education.
- Research colleges and universities that offer a program in my

major area of study. This research can be conducted through visits to my local library, through a search on the Internet, and by talking with representatives in the Human Resource department where I work.

- Determine how I would like to attend classes. Because of my family situation, I will attend locally. I will evaluate the following alternatives:
  a. Attend daytime classes on campus. If I select this alternative, I will need to make arrangements with my employer in order to take the time off of work.
  b. Attend night classes on campus or through extension locations throughout the community.
  c. Complete the degree through correspondence courses.
  d. Attend classes on-line from my home via the Internet.
- Select the colleges that best meet my criteria.
- Gather transcripts from my previous education.
- Send applications to these colleges.

Marcia might also have a concurrent action plan describing the preparations she will make in order to make this goal a priority. This will include a plan for making the time available to study, a plan describing how she will handle her other top priorities, and possibly a list of things she will no longer do. She will also have a long-term action plan in place with some broadly defined steps to help her to meet her goal of receiving her bachelor's degree by her thirtieth birthday.

4. Stephanie is a marketing communications manager for a large company. Her goal is to be promoted within her company to a higher-level marketing communications position within the next year. Her tentative action plan might contain the following steps:

- Each day, visualize myself in my new office making decisions that are typical of higher-level marketing communications professionals.
- Determine what I don't already know about marketing communications in my company, and learn it.

- Continue to do an excellent job in my current position.
- Inform my supervisor that I want to make even stronger contributions to the company in the area of marketing communications and that I am interested in advancing within this area. Ask for her advice on how I can best do this. Be ready to give some suggestions for enhancing marketing communications.
- Request informational interviews with higher level marketing communications people to learn more about the field and their backgrounds. Prepare an agenda and a list of questions for these interviews before scheduling the first one.
- Repeat these steps until I receive the promotion.

Once Jane, Eva, Marcia, and Stephanie have developed their action plans, they can include the appropriate steps in their prioritized daily action plans. This will help them to ensure that they are working on their high-priority goals each day. You can do this, too.

What are your action steps for achieving your goals? If you have not yet written them, do it now. When you develop your action plan, you will want to consider how suitable it is to you and your situation, the amount of time required to complete each step, any outside forces or influences that might affect the plan, and your commitment to the plan.

As you are taking action, you are making decisions. Everything you do in life requires decisions. You make a decision to get out of bed in the morning. You decide what to wear, whether you should put gas in the car now or wait until it is almost empty, whether to make a phone call, what to buy at the supermarket, and what to eat for dinner tonight. When there may be several alternative actions for a situation or if the action will have a major impact on your life, you might want to engage in a decision analysis. In one of the sample action plans described earlier, Marcia might have engaged in a decision analysis to determine the class attendance plan that best fit her situation.

After having been a Minnesota state systems analyst for four years, I engaged in a decision analysis after setting a goal to learn

more about business by working as a systems analyst in a nongov-
ernment organization. My goal was to find a new position within
the next month. I had three prerequisites for this position:

- The salary for this position must be at least as much as my
  current salary.
- The position must be in an IBM mainframe environment, where
  COBOL was the major programming language used.
- The location where I would work must be within driving dis-
  tance of my current home.

I started by responding to local newspaper ads and contacting
a local information systems search firm. My efforts resulted in interviews at four companies and job offers from all four of them
within a week. All four met my three prerequisites. I asked the human resource manager at each company for one week to think about
the offer before responding. They all agreed. During this time, I
performed a decision analysis using the following process, which
will also work for you when you are choosing from among several
alternatives.

Step 1:
On a piece of paper, draw a chart showing the alternative decisions
(in this case, the four job offers) across the top and the decision-
making criteria along the left side. Under each alternative, leave
room for two columns that will be used later in this analysis. (See
Appendix B for a sample chart.)

I listed the four companies along the top. On the left side, I
listed criteria such as initial salary, benefits package, types of projects
that would be assigned to me, opportunity for advancement, college
tuition reimbursement program, working environment, my comfort
level with the interviewer, reputation of the company, driving dis-
tance from my home, cost of parking, etc.

Step 2:
For each criterion, assign a weight between one and five and write
this weight next to the criterion.

I gave salary a weight of "2," since my prerequisite was that the salary had to be at least equal to my current salary. All offers were more than my current salary, and they were all within four percent of each other. A larger weight would have skewed this to be more important than it was to me at the time. I went on to weight the benefits package a "4," types of projects a "5," etc.

Step 3:

Evaluate each alternative for each criterion by assigning a score between 0 and 5, with "5" meaning the alternative very highly meets the criterion and "0" meaning that the alternative does not at all meet the criterion. Write the score in the cell (the box at the cross-section of the alternative and the criterion).

When I went through this step, I gave the first company a "3," the second company a "4," the third company a "4," and the fourth company a "3" for initial salary. The first company had an excellent benefits package, and I gave it a "5" in this area. I gave a score of "4" to each of the other companies for benefits. I then went on to score each of the criteria for each of the companies.

Step 4:

Multiply the weight of the criterion by the score of the criterion for each alternative. Write this number in a separate column under each alternative.

I made sure that I had two columns under each company, one for the score and the other for the score multiplied by the weight. I performed the calculations and entered them on my chart.

Step 5:

Add the weighted scores for each alternative.

I performed this calculation, which gave me one total for each company.

Step 6:

Compare the totals. (If one of the totals is significantly higher than the others, this is the alternative that best meets the criteria. If there is not a significant difference between the highest total and the second highest total, you can either make a judgment call or add more criteria.)

From my decision analysis, I was able to determine that the offer from 3M was the one that best fit my criteria.

—— —— ——

I stayed with 3M for more than twenty-six years, had opportunities to develop and to make significant contributions, and was promoted throughout the ranks to the top one-half of one percent of the more than 75,000 employees. These facts demonstrated to me that it was well worth the time I took many years ago to perform a simple decision analysis to determine which job offer to accept.

In addition to requiring decisions, actions also involve risks. Because of their fear of taking risks, some women do not take the action necessary to be successful. If they thought about it, they would realize that they take risks in everything they do, from walking across a street, to applying for a job, to getting married.

One of the reasons that some women avoid taking risks is their fear of failure. Many of the successful women interviewed for this book said that they did not look at failure as failure, but as a learning opportunity.

We have all engaged in these learning opportunities during our lives. Willie Jolley discusses success and failure in the following excerpt from *A Setback Is a Setup for a Comeback*:

> You failed many times, although you may not remember. The first time you tried to walk, you fell down. The first time you tried to talk, you hardly made a sound. The first time you dressed yourself, you may have looked like a clown. But you didn't give up! Did you hit the ball the first time you swung a bat? Did you make a cartwheel the first time you tried that? Did you jerk the car the first time you drove a stick? Did you do it perfectly the first time you tried a magic trick? Heavy hitters, the ones who hit the most home runs, also strike out the most, when all is said and done. Babe Ruth struck out 1,330 times, but he also

hit 714 home runs. R.H. Macy failed seven times before his store in New York caught on. We all fail sometimes; it is part of success. Just don't stop trying! Don't worry about failure. Worry about the chances you miss when you don't even try.

To be successful, it is necessary to take risks. According to an old proverb, "Progress always involves risks. You can't steal second while keeping one foot on first." The Olympic gold medalist, Jean Claude Killy, said, "In order to win, you must risk loss."

In setting goals and developing action plans, a woman can determine the risk involved by determining the following factors:

- The probability of success
- The benefits of success
- The probability of failure
- The consequence of failure

After evaluating these factors, a woman can then determine whether she can decrease the risk and still reach her goal. One of my university professors once stated, "There is risk in crossing the street, but you can lessen it considerably by keeping your eyes open." Reduce the risk, and increase the probability of success.

These "Ten Commandments of Risk Taking," from an unknown source, put it into perspective:

- Thou shalt know that all growth requires risk.
- Thou shalt take into consideration all options.
- Thou shalt be willing to feel uncomfortable and look foolish.
- Thou shalt seek emotional support.
- Thou shalt be willing to pay the price.
- Thou shalt know that it is okay to change your mind.
- Thou shalt know that being rejected is not the worst thing that will happen to you.
- Thou shalt be willing to be without answers.
- Thou shalt know that if you don't try, you will never know.
- Thou shalt know that life is all too short and very precious. Trust your heart.

Sometimes taking action requires problem-solving skills. Some problems are simple and can be solved easily without extensive thought or analysis. Others are more complex and require the use of a process. The following problem-solving process works well for many successful women:

1. Write a synopsis of the current situation, clearly describing the problem. Be as objective as possible.
2. Determine the root cause of the problem. This might start with a list of probable causes. Take into consideration that the problem may be a symptom of another problem and that there can be more than one root cause.
3. Evaluate the root cause to determine what can be changed.
4. Brainstorm alternative solutions for solving the problem.
5. Evaluate each of the alternative solutions.
6. Select and implement the best alternative.

By making decisions, developing action plans, taking risks, and solving problems, successful women have been able to take the action necessary to become even more successful. They know that they need to act in order to accomplish their goals. Taking the first step in an action plan starts the momentum to continued action and to success.

CHAPTER

Stay Focused!

While being flexible

Success requires concentration and focus on our vision, priorities, and goals. However, ours is a time of shrinking concentration spans and less focus. Why are people focusing less now than before? I asked a cross section of business people, both women and men, what they thought. Following are some of their answers regarding their opinions of reasons for less concentration and shorter attention spans:

- "There are so many communication devices that interrupt a person's time. We have cell phones, pagers, call waiting, Internet instant messages, etc."
- "We are constantly rushing from one activity to another, without a moment in between. This does not allow for periods of exploration in the woods, fishing, taking a walk, or just concentration."
- "In our hurry-up world of fragmented communications, we have become accustomed to multi-tasking."
- "Information is available in so many different sources and in so many different forms today. This includes print (newspa-

pers, magazines, books), broadcast (television and radio), online (Internet and email), and personal interaction."

- "The invention of the television remote control has enabled us to shorten our attention span."

- "Television and movies are edited to move quickly. This reflects an aesthetic style, and it also reflects the faster and faster pace of the world at large."

- "When I see the movies and cartoons that kids watch today, they almost make me nervous just watching them! So full of noise, speed, and special effects, they are aimed at getting the kids' adrenaline pumped. With a steady diet of this, kids get bored easily with things that might require a longer attention span. Many young adults have grown up with this and have known it to be a way of life ever since they can remember."

- "In my situation, I sometimes have so much on my mind that I have a difficult time clearing it to concentrate on a project. If my mind is cluttered, I become more nervous and frustrated. This then leads to lack of concentration and a shorter attention span. I concentrate better when my mind is relaxed."

- "Because people are always rushing, they have more difficulty compartmentalizing their lives today. They bring work home at night and try to do this while spending time with the family, reading the junk mail, doing the chores around the house, watching TV, and answering phone calls. While at work they make personal phone calls and plan their home schedules. They are trying to concentrate on several different tasks simultaneously."

- "People instinctively value and reward instant response today, from fast foods to Web ordering to e-business. The situation is driven and exacerbated by an information overload world. This sets up a huge pull to be in reactive mode most of the time, making reflection available only to those who can mentally propel themselves out of the fray."

- "The intake of more caffeine and more sugar contributes to less concentration."

- "Today, the family system is on the go constantly, conditioning us to move fast and not take time for reflection or focus."

Although some of the businesspeople conceded that it is conceivable that shorter attention spans may help people to do several things simultaneously and keep pace with today's rapidly changing world, they all agreed that concentration and focus were ultimately necessary for personal and professional success.

The preceding chapters have highlighted successes of some of the women interviewed for this book. All of these women have focused on their priorities, goals, and action steps to create success in their lives. When Nancy Albertini was developing her executive search firm, she focused on her financial objectives, as well as her goal to enhance people's lives. When Laurie Windham founded her consulting company, she focused on the niche of the market that she could best serve. When Kathy White decided to go back to school, she focused on her education and didn't stop until she had her doctorate degree.

Alexander Hamilton once said, "Men give me credit for genius. All the genius I have lies in this: When I have a subject in hand, I study it profoundly. Day and night, it is before me. I explore it in all its bearings. My mind becomes pervaded with it. Then . . . people are pleased to call [the effort that I made] the fruit of genius. It is the fruit of labor and thought." It is the fruit of focus and concentration.

I first met Connie Wolf in Brussels, Belgium, where she was the European vice president of human resources and communications for Dow Corning. She had lived in Europe for almost seven years at that time. In college, she had majored in marketing. During her career, she had been in advertising, communications, consumer and industrial marketing, human resources, and organization development. I was just as impressed with her soft-spoken manner as I was with the breadth of her experience and her business success.

Although Connie's career included many different functions, she always focused on in-depth studying and learning about the area in which she was currently assigned. "I liked to be grounded in it," she said. "This helped me to develop the expertise needed to do the job well." Being "grounded" and focused on her mission, priorities, and goals also helps a woman to be recognized by receiving expanded responsibilities and promotions.

Dr. Jeanne Elnadry is another woman who focuses on her priorities and goals and, thus, has achieved success. Her parents encouraged her to be all that she could be. They encouraged their children, both boys and girls, to seek a trade or profession, whichever they chose. As an adult, Jeanne decided to be a nurse and pursued this career direction. It wasn't until she had been a nurse for several years that she decided she would rather give orders than simply carry them out. It was then that she determined that she really wanted to be a doctor.

Once she had made her decision to be a doctor, Jeanne focused on this goal despite the personal hardships she endured along the path. Since she had finished her nursing degree ten years earlier, the other medical school students were younger. Because of this, she thought they were better able to concentrate on their studies. "I had been out of school for quite some time, had not been studying, and wasn't in the mode for that kind of academic work," she said. After failing her first exam, she told herself, "I just have to work harder. I can do this." She worked to improve her concentration and graduated with honors at the top of her class. She is now a physician specializing in internal medicine. She and another physician have a medical practice in Yuma, Arizona, where they are so successful that, after only two years, they could not accept any new patients.

When asked about the importance of focus and concentration in her life, Jeanne says, "It's very important to me, but it doesn't mean staying focused only on my career. It means staying focused on what is important in my life, which includes career as well as my other priorities. It is critical, though difficult, to identify the most important activities and focus on those first."

In today's complicated world, multiple distractions vie for our attention at any given time. The way in which we deal with these distractions determines how well we are able to focus on our goals and priorities. If you will take the time during the next twenty-four hours to observe how you handle distractions, you might have some surprises. During this time period, write each distraction as it occurs. After recording a distraction on paper, write a comment on how you handle this distraction. At the end of the twenty-four hours, review your notes, observe any patterns that may exist, congratulate yourself for the times that you handled the distraction well, and determine where you can make some improvements.

Following are some methods that successful women use to handle distractions:

- Set aside quiet time during the day to focus on your top priorities or action steps. During these quiet times, stay away from the telephone and other sources of interruption, allowing interruptions only for emergencies.
- Decrease the stress in your body and your mind by practicing the relaxation exercise in Chapter 2 before you start focusing on a priority or action step.
- Keep a piece of paper and a pen at hand while you are concentrating on a project or task. When an unrelated thought enters your mind, write it down. These thoughts can be reviewed at a later time.
- Periodically during the next month, repeat the exercise of recording your distractions and the methods that you use to deal with them. Note the progress that you are making in this area.

Bobbie Stevens has accomplished every goal that she has set for herself. She said, "I discovered a process for releasing stress and strengthening the mind/body system. This process has brought me to a totally different level of functioning. It brought me to a higher level of health, energy, and self-confidence." Bobbie's process includes relaxation, visualization, and yoga-type exercises. She stresses that it is important for us to visualize what we want and to keep our attention focused on it, no matter what happens. In her course, Bobbie teaches several methods for improving our ability to focus.

As we can condition, strengthen and tone our bodies, we can also condition and strengthen our minds to improve our concentration and focus. The keys to increasing our ability to focus are practice and repetition. The following exercises will help to improve your ability to concentrate and to focus on your priorities and goals:

1. Focus on an object.

Select an object in the room that is pleasing to you. This could be a painting, a sculpture, a piece of furniture, etc. Move your chair so that you can see the object clearly without any physical strain. Sit comfortably with your back straight. Now fix your eyes on the object, and leave them there. Focus your full attention on the object for three minutes. Do not let other thoughts distract you during the three minutes. If your mind starts to wander, bring it back to focus on the object.

Keep a piece of paper and a pencil on hand during this exercise. Each time your mind wanders from the object, you can then make a tick mark on the paper. If you are like most of us, there will be lots of tick marks on your paper after you complete the exercise for the first time. However, the number of tick marks should decrease as you strengthen your ability to focus by repeating this exercise during the next several days.

2. Candle concentration.

Bobbie Stevens teaches the candle concentration exercise in her course. In order to do this one, you will need a lighted candle. Start by sitting comfortably, as described previously, and place the lighted candle on a table about three feet in front of you. Gaze directly into the flame of the candle (blinking as necessary) for two minutes. Then close your eyes, and press the palms of your hands lightly against your eyelids. When you close your eyes, you will retain the image of the flame. Concentrate on that image, and do not let the flame wander or disappear. If it should disappear, bring it back simply by looking for it (keeping your eyes closed). Keep your palms pressed against your closed eyes for an additional two minutes.

This exercise not only helps to improve focus and concentration, but it also brings restfulness and relaxation. This, in turn, helps to relieve stress. By decreasing stress, a person is better able to focus.

3. Physical exercise.

Another way to clear the mind and increase the ability to concentrate is through physical exercise. In the past, I had days that it seemed like it would be a major effort to walk to my car and drive home after work. I would feel so tired that I thought I needed a nap. The fact was that I really needed some physical exercise. After sitting in an office all day, making decisions, and handling major problems, I felt tired. My ability to focus seemed to be gone for the day. At first, it surprised me how a twenty-minute walk could make such a big difference and eliminate these symptoms.

Physical exercise allows the mind to relax. It releases stress, which is a major barrier to concentration. In addition, it helps to strengthen the body.

—— —— ——

In *Brain Building*, Marilyn vos Savant says, "When there is a severe decline in memory and mental function, it is usually caused by such diseases as Alzheimer's which affects only twenty percent of the very old. Most of the other decline, the kind that people tend to fret about as they age, is now believed to be caused by the lack of mental exercise."

My ability to focus has definitely helped me to accomplish my goals and to enjoy success in all areas of my life. My European position was a developmental assignment, which allowed me to learn as well as to accomplish objectives which I was given the liberty to recommend to the company. During the two years I spent in Europe, it would have been very easy to get a flavor of European cultures and business life and still not show concrete results for my efforts in my job there. When I first knew that I would have the assignment, I decided that I was going to focus on three or four areas and to make major contributions in these areas. I selected the following four areas:

- Sales and marketing productivity, which involved restructuring internal job descriptions to best meet customer requirements. This would be demonstrated by conducting a pilot in one business unit in one country.
- Sales support systems, which included introducing computers to sales personnel to assist them in becoming more effective and more efficient in their jobs.
- Customer satisfaction measurement, which also involved the implementation of improvements, based on customer requirements.
- Balanced scorecard development, which included various measures that would be used to determine the progress of all business units in Europe.

For each of these four areas of concentration, I established teams, conducted research, developed plans, and started implementation. Of course, there were other projects that came up while I was in Europe that threatened my ability to focus on my selected priorities. Some of them were quite attractive, and I found myself wishing that I was two people and could do more; however, I was able to analyze the priority in each case and to concentrate on the established priorities. At the end of the two years, I had accomplished my objectives and was promoted to a new position in the company.

Along with increasing your ability to focus comes a paradox. Even though it is extremely important to focus on your goals and action steps, it is also important to be flexible. In some cases, we may have conflicting priorities. In others, several of our priorities might need our attention simultaneously. During these times, an analysis will help to determine what is the most important thing to be doing at the moment.

Nancy Albertini talks about a slight recession that occurred in her industry a few years after she founded her executive search firm. "We came out of that downturn very successfully," she said. "It was because we focused. We said this is what we're good at, and this is where we should concentrate our efforts." She added that, in any business, the market is continuing to evolve and that a good businessperson always needs to consider alternate paths.

Nancy cites several examples of how many large companies were not ready for the Internet and the new way of doing business through this channel. She stresses the importance of being focused, but not *too* focused so as to lose opportunities in a new market. She said, "You have to constantly be open to new ideas. If you're not, you're going to be behind."

Keeping in mind that we need to be flexible, let's work more on focusing on our visions, priorities, goals, and action steps. In addition to increasing our concentration, this feeds the subconscious mind the information it needs to help us to be successful.

Before the 1993 Superbowl, Dallas Cowboys coach Jimmy Johnson gave his team a pep talk. He told them that, if he laid a two-by-four plank on the floor, each of them would walk across it and not fall. The reason for this would be that their focus would be on walking the plank. "But if I put the same two-by-four ten stories high between two buildings," said Johnson, "only a few would make it." This would be because the focus would be on falling. He told his team not to focus on the crowd, the media, or the possibility of losing. Instead, they were to focus on each play of the game, just as if it were a good practice session. The Dallas Cowboys won the game 52 to 17.

If we focus on winning, we will win. If we focus on accomplishing our goals, we will accomplish them. If we focus on success, we will be successful. The key is to focus and to continue to improve our ability to focus through the exercises in this chapter.

CHAPTER

Remain Positive, No Matter What!

Opening doors with a winning attitude

Thoughts direct energy. Positive thoughts create positive energy and results, and negative thoughts create negative energy and results. If you expect the best, you are more likely to achieve it.

In order to see this for yourself, look around you at the positive, optimistic people that you know. Are they successful? Chances are that they are enjoying life and creating what they want in their lives.

Now look at the negative, pessimistic people that you know. How successful are they? My guess is that they are not happy with their lives.

How happy are you with your life? Are you as successful as you would like to be? How positive are you? Do you look at problems as problems, or do you look at them as opportunities? Oil magnate and philanthropist John D. Rockefeller maintained that he tried to turn every disaster into an opportunity, and it certainly paid off for him!

We all have problems and challenges in life, and many people feel defeated by these. Our attitude and the way that we handle our problems and challenges will contribute to our success or lack thereof. Dr. Norman Vincent Peale addresses this in the following excerpt from *The Power of Positive Thinking*:

> Altogether too many people are defeated by the everyday problems of life. They go struggling, perhaps even whining, through their days with a sense of dull resentment at what they consider the "bad breaks" life has given them. In a sense, there may be such a thing as "the breaks" in this life, but there is also a spirit and method by which we can control and even determine those breaks. It is a pity that people should let themselves be defeated by the problems, cares, and difficulties of human existence, and it is also quite unnecessary.
>
> In saying this, I certainly do not ignore or minimize the hardships and tragedies of the world, but neither do I allow them to dominate. You can permit obstacles to control your mind to the point where they are uppermost and thus become the dominating factors in your thought pattern. By learning how to cast them from the mind, by refusing to become mentally subservient to them, and by channeling spiritual power through your thoughts, you can rise above obstacles which ordinarily might defeat you. You need be defeated only if you are willing to be.

As I interviewed successful women for this book, I asked each of them about her experiences with failure in her life. Some would say that they had never failed. Others would hesitate before answering, as if they were trying of think of an example. Finally they would mention something that had happened—losing a spelling bee, being dismissed from a job assignment, failing a test, getting a divorce. Each of them maintained that they perceived of these occurrences as learning opportunities rather than failures. Many of them talked about the lessons they had learned that enabled them to accomplish greater goals. One woman said that it was because of her failures that she was able to become successful.

William James said, "The greatest discovery of my generation is that human beings can alter their lives by altering their attitudes of mind."

My personal experience validates this philosophy. Before I decided to alter my attitude, I spent much time in hospitals. Early in my career, I was diagnosed with a serious heart condition. My doctor ordered me to quit work, as he said that my heart condition was too serious for me to contend with the stress of a job. At the time, I was twenty-nine years old and was concerned about the possibility of not living to see my thirtieth birthday. I was even more concerned about the possibility of not having the opportunity to raise my children, who were then eight and two. Even though I enjoyed my work, I chose to follow the doctor's orders.

During the next several months, more was discovered about my particular heart condition. With the use of a combination of four different medications, the condition was under control. I was gradually able to return to work, first part time and then full time. However, worry and concern about the heart condition still permeated my existence.

Less than two weeks after returning to work full time, I had an experience that helped me to realize the power of thought. While sitting at my desk, I started hearing a constant ringing sound and was not able to determine the source of this sound. As the ringing started to get louder, I decided to discuss it with a colleague. When I arrived at his desk, he was not there. His phone was ringing, so I answered it with the intent of taking a message for him. To my alarm, the voice at the other end of the line was garbled. This was a sign to me that the ringing I had been hearing was coming from inside my head, and something was terribly wrong. I politely told the person on the phone that we had a bad connection and suggested that she call back in a few minutes when my colleague was due to return. To verify that I was correct in the diagnosis of the problem, I dialed the phone number of the recorded time and temperature message. The sound from the message was also garbled.

My next sensation was a light-headed feeling. I called my doctor, who suggested that I have someone drive me home, that I go directly to bed, and that I call him the next morning if I had not improved. By the time I got home, I was completely deaf in my right ear. Thinking that this would pass, I waited until morning to call the doctor. At that point, I was so dizzy that I could not lift my head off my pillow without being sick to my stomach. I remember being barely conscious as someone wheeled a gurney from the hospital emergency room to the back of the station wagon where I was lying. I heard a voice saying, "Be careful with her. She is very, very sick."

I lay in a hospital bed for almost three weeks, not able to move because of the extreme dizziness. Once I could get up, it took months to learn to walk a straight line again. I never regained my hearing. The doctors explained that a blood vessel in my inner ear had "shorted out," causing the inner ear to die and destroying the balance mechanism. They attributed this to stress. In looking back, I know now that the stress was self-inflicted by my worries about my health.

After a while I was again able to return to work but was in and out of hospitals for several years for various health problems, including asthma, pneumonia, heart irregularities, and abdominal surgeries. When I finally started to think positively about my health and my life, I became healthy. I am still deaf in the right ear but have learned to compensate for this. My asthma is under control, and I no longer need to take medication for my heart. There definitely is power in positive thinking! I had altered my health, and my life, by altering my "attitude of mind."

Following are nine methods for improving one's attitude and outlook. They have contributed to my success and to the success of other women (and men).

1. Refrain from the three C's.

During the course that Bobbie Stevens developed, she and her husband Dean teach the "square tongue rule." Dean states this rule quite simply when he advises course participants to refrain from the three C's—complaining, criticizing, and condemning. He recommends that participants become aware of each time they complain, criticize, or condemn. He then suggests that, while taking the course, the person gently bite the end of her tongue as a reminder each time she engages in one of the three C's. He jokingly adds that, if the tip of the tongue is bitten too many times, it might be bitten off; hence the "square tongue rule."

When I first heard about the "square tongue rule," I almost dismissed it. My initial thought was that I don't complain, criticize, or condemn. However, since I was committed to get as much out of this course as possible, I decided to follow Dean's instructions for the next week. As I became more aware of my words and thoughts, I learned that I wasted a great deal of time making critical remarks. At first I would justify my remarks to myself by thinking, "I'm not criticizing, but just stating a fact." I discovered how easy it is to justify our thoughts, words, and actions. It became apparent that I needed to make some adjustments in my thinking.

After some analysis, I realized that not only do the three C's rob our time, but they also drag us down into a spiral of negativity. The messages, which they send to the subconscious mind, inhibit our success. Although it took some time for me to progress in eliminating the three C's from my life, I discovered that it was well worth the effort.

During the next week, I suggest that you become aware of each time that you complain, criticize or condemn. When you catch yourself engaging in any of these C's, ask yourself what you would need to do in order to restate or eliminate your current thought or words. If you are like I was, you might discover that you are complaining, criticizing, or condemning more than you would have thought you were. However, as you observe this and restate your thoughts, you'll soon find that you are engaging in the three C's less often. By doing this, you will be eliminating the negative energy that is generated by complaining, criticizing, and condemning.

By eliminating complaining, criticizing, and condemning, we become more positive. On the mental level, positive attracts positive, and negative attracts negative. Positive thoughts help to attract more positive experiences into our lives. This begins an upward spiral. As we begin to see things in a more positive way, we become more positive. As we become more positive, we increase our potential for success.

2. Eliminate worry from your life.

Just as most successful women do not waste time complaining, criticizing, and condemning, they also do not waste time worrying. They realize that worry not only generates negative energy, but it also does not make the source of the worry any better.

There are so many things that can be sources of worry in our lives. We grew up worrying about whether we would pass a test or if we would have a date for the prom. Many of us were conditioned to worry, and we just kept worrying our way into adulthood. In addition to health issues, these worries might be about whether we will have enough money to pay our bills, whether our children will do well in school, whether the new boss will be happy with our work, or if we will be on time for an appointment.

Before Cliff and I were engaged, I was worried that he may have another heart attack. When I didn't hear from him at the beginning of a day, it would affect my thoughts on other things. Of course, Cliff sensed my anxiety, and this did not enhance our relationship. When I finally decided to stop worrying, our relationship blossomed, my mind became more clear for positive thoughts, I became more productive, people noticed my more positive attitude, and I was promoted at work. I learned that I could care, but that did not mean that I needed to worry.

Many of us have serious concerns, such as life-threatening illnesses in our families. Worrying does not cure an illness, and we ourselves can become sick from the worry. Once we decide to stop worrying, we are better able to handle a situation that might have been the object of our worry. During the next week, you might want to observe whether you are spending time worrying. If you discover that you are worrying, you can then give some thought to what you can do to continue caring and stop worrying.

3. Put on a happy face.

Have you ever noticed how people seem to want to please you more when you smile at them? To me, they appear to be more friendly and outgoing. When I realized this, I started to consciously observe people's reactions as I smiled at them while walking through the long corridors of 3M's office complex. I discovered that, whenever I smiled, the recipient of the smile would return the smile. This, in turn, lifted my spirits. As a result, my smile became more genuine as I met the next person.

In her course, Bobbie Stevens teaches the power of positive thinking. After my management group decided to participate in the course, a colleague told me of a conversation she had had with the manager of another department. The colleague had mentioned to the manager that my group would be attending this course. She was amused by the reaction when the manager said, "Oh no! This means that we will have ten more 'Joans' running around, smiling at people, looking through their rose-colored glasses, and getting all of the promotions! I wish I could be like that."

The truth is that she could be like that. The formula is simple. As one of my philosopher friends said, "We don't see things as they are; we see them as we are." If we convey an attitude of happiness and show this through our smiles, we will see the same thing in other people. This is illustrated by the story of a man who traveled from town to town looking for a place to start his business. As he went into one community, he asked a resident about the type of people who lived there. The wise resident asked him what type of people lived in the town that he was leaving. The man replied that the people were unfriendly, argumentative, and uncooperative. The resident replied that the man would find the people in this town the same as the ones in the place the man had left. The next day, another man arrived in the same town and asked the same resident about the type of people who lived in the town. The resident asked this man the same question about the type of people in the town he was leaving. This man replied that the people were friendly, cooperative, and always willing to help. The resident answered his question by saying that he would find that the people in this town were the same as the ones in the town that he had left. Both men had visited the same town, had talked with the same resident, and had asked the same question; however they had received different answers, depending on how each of them saw things.

Remember, a smile is contagious and therefore can change our lives. In my experience this is absolutely true.

4. Look for the good in everything.

At a 3M meeting several years ago, I met a woman named Mary, who was the ultimate for making lemonade when life dealt her lemons. I had never before known anyone with an attitude as positive as hers. At the beginning of the meeting, each of us introduced ourselves and gave a synopsis of the reasons for our participation in this series of meetings. Mary had recently moved to St. Paul, Minnesota, from Washington, D.C. She had rented an apartment about twenty-five miles from the office where she worked. She talked about how fantastic it was to have an hour-long commute to and from her new job, as she was able to see much of the city and to listen to motivating tapes while she was driving.

Shortly after the move, her new position in St. Paul was eliminated. She told us that, even though she had enjoyed this job, losing it was a wonderful opportunity to learn more about the company by looking at other positions and to determine what she would like to do next. Others who heard her told me later that they didn't think Mary was "for real." As I got to know her, though, I realized that she was truly genuine. As others in the group began to know her, they also realized it and strived to be more like her. They recognized that she was attracting positive results into her life through her attitude. When I was hiring people for my next new department, Mary was one of the first people I hired. Her attitude and enthusiasm were contagious, and she contributed significantly to the success of this department.

In *Golden Nuggets*, Sir John Templeton says, "By choosing to look for the good in all situations, we can place our attention on workable solutions to problems, rather than focusing on what we perceive as wrong."

I once attended a class given by a chiropractor who had developed an excellent chiropractic procedure, which not only included adjustments, but also nutrition and "forgiveness." During the class sessions, he discussed the subconscious mind and the fact that thought precedes action, even physical action/reaction within our bodies.

This wise doctor of chiropractic explained that the secret to recovery in many of these cases was forgiveness. Sometimes unknowingly, we carry grudges for something that happened to us at sometime during our lives. If we do some serious soul-searching, we can determine if there might be someone that we have not forgiven. In class, we learned the three steps of forgiveness:

1. Forgive the person who may have wronged us.
2. Forgive ourselves for carrying the grudge, whether it was inten tional or unintentional.
3. Look for the good in whatever it was that happened to us. This is the most difficult step, but it is necessary for the process to work.

There were some people in the class who were very ill and had traveled to doctors throughout the country in search of cures for their illnesses. It seemed to me that I saw miracles occurring that week when many of these ill people were relieved of their symptoms. In following up after the class, I learned that, for most of these people, the symptoms never returned.

During the class, I determined that part of the reason I have had abdominal cramps most of my life went back to a violent situation that I had witnessed when I was twelve years old. I had not realized that I had carried a grudge against someone for causing this situation. Even though the perpetrator was no longer living, I was still carrying this grudge, and the violent act was still living in my subconscious mind. After engaging in the three steps of forgiveness for twenty-four hours, I still had abdominal cramps. It was then that I realized that I was merely going through the motions. I had to do some real work to genuinely forgive and to look for some good in the violent situation that had occurred. This gave me an opportunity to not only forgive, but also to grow. Since that time, I have rarely experienced abdominal cramps.

Looking for the good in all experiences contributes to building a more positive attitude. This excerpt from Dr. Dean Portinga's paper, "Pronounce All Things Good," helps to explain this.

> The act of affirming the good is a very powerful factor, reflecting itself in all areas of our lives. . . . The thought of good dissolves all kinds of beliefs in burdens. This thought of good dissolves suspicion, doubt, fear, ingratitude, self-pity, grudges, sadness, hurt feelings, impatience, hatred, condemnation, revenge, and bitterness. All kinds of negative thoughts that cause burdens in thought, body, and experience can be cleared up with such a simple statement as, "Only good is going on."
>
> When you speak the word "good", you are releasing power. The word "good" is creative. Good is created as fast as good thoughts and words are spoken. When you speak forth the word "good", you evolve, stir up, and release good to manifest.
>
> The word "good" is also self-increasing. When you speak forth words of good, you not only create good, but that good continues to create more good. It is self-multiplying. Thus, by speaking words of good, you first create and then increase all things good in your experience. This includes the physical well-being, financial well-being, and the well-being of human relationships. Good is another name for strength and power. . . . You can confidently expect good things to

happen when you take your stand and pronounce everything good!

5. Know that you can do it.

A positive attitude, combined with self-affirmation, contributes to success. If you continually tell yourself that you can accomplish your objectives, you significantly increase the likelihood of doing just that. Dee Ray knew that she could be a very good stockbroker. She not only became an excellent stockbroker, but she later became a senior vice president and investment executive in her company.

Joan T. Smith started her career when a businessperson was called a businessman, a salesrep was called a salesman, and a woman who worked in business was usually a secretary. Joan was career oriented and knew that she could do the same type of job that the men in her company were doing. She became the first female officer in the trust investment department of the bank where she worked, and she excelled at this profession.

Many of the first women to enter the corporate world were pioneers who struggled for each promotion. However, they did this with the knowledge and confidence that they had the ability to do their jobs well. As they proved that women could do jobs that were typically held by men, they paved the way for women who are working in the business world today.

Dr. Jeanne Elnadry was painfully shy as a child. "I did something about it when I was in junior high school," she said. "I remember walking down a hallway one day and feeling so out of place, as teenagers often do. It was like a light went on in my head. I realized that if I wanted to change the situation, I was the one who had to do it. It would not happen by itself. So, during the course of those years, I worked for the school newspaper. I started out as a reporter and learned how to talk with people. I joined the drill team and eventually became its captain. These were structured activities that helped me to deal with the shyness and get beyond it. I think that the attitude of trying to get beyond a difficulty is what kept me going."

Once she realized why she felt out of place, Jeanne knew that she could do what was necessary to overcome her shyness. She is now a successful physician.

Know that you can accomplish your objectives. In some cases, it will take additional education or training. In others, it might mean negotiating. In still others, it might mean changing some habits. If you know that you can accomplish your objectives and commit yourself to take the necessary steps, you will be successful.

6. Laugh.

A growing number of doctors and nurses are studying the healing power of humor. Various studies have indicated that laughter can stimulate a hormone that increases immune response. I read about this shortly before I injured my back on a business trip. Since the back injury was so painful, I went to see a doctor after I arrived at my destination. He prescribed medication for pain and to relax my muscles. He also suggested that I stay in bed for the next two days. I took the medication immediately and returned to my hotel. The back pain was worse the next day, so much so that it prevented me from attending my meetings. I was in bed feeling sorry for myself when I remembered the passage I had read about laughter. I began to laugh. I flipped through the TV channels looking for a situation comedy. I thought of funny stories, and I laughed more. The more I laughed, the better I felt. I could still feel the pain, but it was no longer dominating my thoughts. By the next day, I was able to attend meetings. The pain was almost gone, even though I had stopped taking the pain medication.

There is healing power in laughter, and this power can heal us mentally and emotionally, as well as physically. Laughter helps to release stress. After a long day at the office, a good laugh will revitalize me. It brings with it a good feeling, a feeling of lightness, a feeling of joy. I also find it enjoyable to spend time with people who have a sense of humor. It is difficult to have a good sense of humor and a bad attitude.

We once had a speaker come to our office and talk to the employees about stress management. He was a medical doctor and was dressed as a clown. As he walked up to the front of the room, some of the employees were wondering how this silly person was able to come to our conservative company to speak to us. By the middle of his talk, everyone in the audience was laughing so hard that several of them had tears running down their faces. At the end of his speech the doctor/clown received a standing ovation. Our departmental productivity increased significantly over the next several days because of his impact.

There is power in laughter. The great entertainer, Bob Hope, said, "I have seen what a good laugh can do. It can transform tears into hope."

7. Value other people.

Each individual on this earth is a miracle. Each of us has unique skills, talents, and aptitudes. We all live in a connected Universe and contribute to the growth of one another. We are partners in the creation of good for all of us. As we show respect for others as individuals, we in turn gain respect.

William Penn wrote, "I expect to pass through life but once. If therefore, there be any kindness I can show, or any good thing that I can to do to any fellow being, let me do it now, and not defer or neglect it, as I shall not pass this way again." Although this was written a long time ago, it helps me to get my life back in perspective each time I read it.

People are so precious, even those who seem to be cross and ornery or who seem to stand in the way of our achieving our objectives. If we value them and show that we care about them as people, we might be surprised at the difference we will see in them. By adjusting our attitude toward them, we might see a change in their attitude toward us. Popular motivational speaker Zig Ziglar says, "You can have everything in life you want, if you will just help enough other people get what they want." Many people just want to know that they are valued and that you respect and care about them.

Connie Wolf, former European vice president of human resources and communications for Dow Corning, advises women who want to create success in their lives to "be kind." It helps maintain our relationships if we ask ourselves if the current situation will really matter tomorrow, next week, or next year.

Another tip from Connie is to make a difference in other's lives. She says that if you believe that you can make a difference for just one person each day through a smile, a kind word, or a helping hand, you yourself will benefit.

It takes very little to touch another person's life, to let people know that you value them. A word of encouragement might make a difference to someone who thinks that it is a lonely and uncaring world. By valuing other people and showing that we care, we are developing a more positive attitude in ourselves.

7. Set an example.

All of us are seen and observed by other people on a daily basis. As we become more successful, it seems that we are "on stage" even more often. Because of my position at 3M, I felt that I was representing the company whenever I was out in public. I would not always know if someone around me would recognize me. Nevertheless, I felt it was important to live my personal standards, regardless of where I might be. People know that I am a positive, optimistic woman. By maintaining this positive attitude, I know I have influenced many others through my example.

Business and management guru Peter Drucker said, "Your first and foremost job as a leader is to raise your own energy level and then to help orchestrate the energies of those around you." This energy includes attitude. It also applies outside of business, as all of us have the opportunity to set an example in our families and communities.

8. Give back to society.

Most of the successful women who participated in my interviews talked about the importance of "giving back." Gayle Crowell gives back when she donates her speaker fees to charity. Nancy Albertini gives back when she focuses her company and her employees on helping to make other people's lives better.

She has founded AngelWorks Foundation through which she has donated one million dollars to various charities. The foundation is spearheading a $20 million fund-raising program for cancer research.

Joan T. Smith enjoyed a successful career as an investment portfolio manager. Now that she is retired, much of her time is spent on giving back. She chairs the finance committee of the American Association for University Women, and she also serves on other local and national committees on a volunteer basis. She is sponsoring a scholarship in the MBA program at the University of Minnesota Carlson School of Management. She said, "It was during a recession that I went back to school for my master's degree. Since I was not working at the time, it was difficult for me financially. By offering this scholarship, I am trying to prevent someone else from going through what I went through."

Giving to others reaps rewards for the giver, even though the giver is not giving for the sake of reward for herself. Ralph Waldo Emerson said, "It is one of the most beautiful compensations of this life that no [woman] can sincerely try to help another without helping [herself]."

— — —

When we are in the midst of challenges and crises, it is sometimes difficult to be optimistic and positive. However, it helps to remember that a positive attitude can open the door to opportunities.

Throughout my career, I have interviewed close to one thousand individuals for jobs within the various organizations that I have managed. Before I interview for a position, I develop a list of criteria and standard questions to ask each interviewee. Regardless of the position, the number one criterion for the position is "Attitude," which is even more important to me than whether the person has the exact technical skills needed for the position. If the interviewee has a positive attitude, I know that he or she can be trained, if need be, on most of the other skills needed for the position. By looking at attitude as the top criteria, I have been able to develop departments that have achieved the following:

- High level of productivity and creativity
- Consistent exceeding of objectives
- High level of morale
- Effective team-building
- High level of respect from others in the company
- Low absenteeism
- Low turnover

The people in these departments have worked hard, and they have worked smart. They have also had fun in doing this. As a result, others in the company have often asked for transfers into these departments. This is due largely to the attitude of the employees.

A positive attitude definitely opens doors. It has for me and for each of the successful women that I have met in my life. It will for you, too.

CHAPTER

Live Your Life with Integrity!

Focusing on what's important

When I lived and worked in Europe, I had two bosses, one in France where I lived and the other in Belgium, the location of our company's European headquarters. Both bosses were women, two of the three highest-ranking women at 3M at that time. I felt fortunate to have the opportunity to learn from these two business giants and was enormously flattered at one point when one of them complimented me by saying that she could always count on my dedication and integrity. She added that, no matter what I say I am going to do, she knows that I will do it. I felt that was the highest compliment that anyone could have paid me. From that day forward, I wanted to make sure that it would always be true.

Maintaining integrity is not easy for many of us. During part of my life, everyday temptations to alter the truth were difficult for me to overcome. When I was in my early thirties, I decided to take up the game of golf. During my first year on the golf course, my scores were sometimes almost twice as high as those of some of my playing partners. Since I was the ultimate perfectionist, this was extremely embarrassing to me. After each hole as we called out our scores, I would be tempted to lower my score by one or two points so that it would not sound quite as bad as it was. A tempting voice inside of me would say, "Make up a number. They probably can't count that high anyway." I would think about it and finally answer the voice, saying, "But I would know it, and I am the one who has to live with myself. If I am concerned about what people will think of me, they are not going to remember my golf scores ten years from now, but they will remember if I lied." The everyday temptations for us to be out of integrity are probably stronger than any other temptations we receive.

All of the successful women to whom I spoke agreed that integrity was of utmost importance to their success. When asked to rate the importance of personal integrity on a scale of one to five, with "five" meaning most important, they all rated it a "five." One said, "Six!" Another said, "Five-five-five!" Following are some of their comments. I hope they will serve to inspire you as you give some consideration to where you see yourself on the personal integrity scale.

- "To be successful, you need to be proud to look yourself in the mirror when you think about how you conduct yourself and how you work with other people. You have to be able to say, 'I'm very proud of what I've done here.' I'm proud of my passion, so I rank that highly. If you can't get personal integrity with what you are doing, then don't do it!" (Nancy Albertini, chief executive officer, Taylor Winfield)

- "You need to be who you are, to be honest, to feel good about yourself, and to be true to yourself. At the end of the day, personal integrity will carry you the whole way." (Gayle Crowell, former president, E.piphany)

- "Part of personal integrity is doing your best. Part of it is being honest. Part of it is being true to your values. People will not remember what you did or what you said, but they will always remember how they felt when they were with you. The way we treat other people is part of our integrity. To succeed, you need to be trustworthy. If we are not honest and we don't keep our integrity, we can't be trustworthy. Another part of it is that sometimes we might be criticized. If we take responsibility for a mistake, a lot of criticism melts away. Part of integrity is taking responsibility for what we have done and acknowledging it. " (Dr. Jeanne Elnadry, physician)

- "If you do not retain your integrity, you end up not liking yourself. If you don't like yourself, it is hard to believe in yourself." (Beth MacDonald, regional franchise director, Asia/Pacific Region, Johnson & Johnson)

- "You have to live with yourself. If you sell your soul to get where you want, it will come back to haunt you in the end. If you don't have respect for yourself, if you can't trust yourself, or if you have done something dishonest, I think it would continue to bother you. It would not make any difference to me how successful I was if I had to do something that wasn't right to get there." (Dee Ray, senior vice president and investment executive, John G. Kinnard and Company)

- "Nothing is worth sacrificing your integrity. It is extremely important to be true to yourself. You need to know what is right for you and to stay on that track." (Dr. Bobbie Stevens, founder and president, Unlimited Futures, L.L.C.)

- "It is important to never compromise the values that you believe are integral to you. Otherwise, you compromise the core of who you are, and then it pulls your foundation out from under you." (Terry Swack, vice president, Experience Design, Razorfish)

- "Integrity is doing what I say I will do and trying to make that almost my whole being. It is about the calls, the follow-up, the calling back if someone is not there, and the follow-through to completion of a task or project. It launched my success the first ten years when

I was more of an individual contributor. After that, personal integrity also became very important in order for people to want to follow me and to do big things." (Dr. Kathy Brittain White, executive vice president and chief information officer, Cardinal Health, Inc.)

One of the interviewees talked about how she had learned the importance of integrity from some traumatic childhood experiences. As a child, she was sexually abused by a relative. She learned later that he had also abused all of her female cousins and, in later years, had tried to molest her daughter. From this horrible experience, she learned that it is very important to be believed and trusted. She said, "Probably the worse thing that can happen now is for someone not to believe me. I have high personal integrity. Even though I will position things to get the best play and achieve the best results, I tell the truth. The reality of how I was treated as a child is so bizarre. Those things are just not normal, and they should not happen. When I look at how everything else was so phenomenal in my life, I wasn't going to let this get to me. On the other hand, it has an impact on how I live my life. Honesty and integrity are so very, very important to me."

What does integrity mean to you? In the case of my golf score, I considered integrity to be an honesty issue. Although honesty contributes to integrity, there are more aspects to integrity than just telling the truth. Integrity is unique for each of us, and most integrity challenges start with details. We might receive early warning signals that we just ignore until they have become a problem.

As you are thinking about your level of integrity, ask yourself the following questions:

- Do I tell the truth?
- Is my word my bond?
- Do my promises have value?
- Do I do what I say I am going to do?
- Am I committed to commitment?

In *The Portable Coach*, Coach University founder Thomas J. Leonard makes the following statement about integrity:

> Everyone, myself included, should be open to micro or macro improvements in how "together" they are. It could be as simple as installing a system that keeps you as up to date as possible in paperwork and organization, so the right responses are always generated quickly.
>
> The same applies to being on the curve, instead of behind it, when it comes to handling taxes, having adequate insurance, being current on registrations and debt repayment, being available in the present moment for key relationships and agreements, and staying rooted in truthfulness and forthrightness.
>
> Integrity is more than just honesty. It's about being integrated, so that all the parts of your life and yourself are cooperating smoothly to honor your best interests. Since we ultimately can't possess anything more important than our good name, any upgrade to your integrity will eventually be an addition to your well-being.

Integrity is the result of having the following three conditions in one's life:

- **Resolution of all important matters**
  This includes the correction of any wrongs, making any personal changes necessary to ensure one's life works well, and fully handling every task and job that one decides to do.

- **Alignment and balance in life**
  Alignment, in this case, means that a person's goals are aligned with her values and priorities, her actions are based on what is true for her, and her commitments are aligned with her vision or purpose in life.

- **Responsibility**
  In speaking about integrity, the word "responsibility" means being responsible for that which occurs in one's life. This includes

handling whatever happens and making necessary adjustments to prevent this type of problem in the future. A responsible person does not blame, complain, or point fingers at other people. She just handles the situation.

By the results she is seeing in her life, it is usually fairly easy for a woman to determine whether she is "in integrity" or "out of integrity." When she is "in integrity," she experiences fewer problems, has consistent feelings of peace and well-being, and she reacts to situations and other people very little. When she is "out of integrity," she is more likely to become distressed and irritable and to blame and criticize others. The more we live our lives with integrity, the more harmony and beauty we will encounter.

In *The Six Pillars of Self Esteem*, Nathaniel Branden says, "One of the greatest deceptions is to tell oneself, 'Only I will know.' Only I will know that I am a liar; only I will know that I deal unethically with people who trust me; only I will know that I have no intention of honoring my promise. The implication is that my judgment is unimportant and that only the judgment of others counts."

In *100 Ways to Motivate Yourself*, Steve Chandler comments on Nathaniel Branden's quote:

> Branden's writing on personal integrity is inspiring because it's directed at creating a happier and stronger self, not at a universal appeal for morality.
>
> One of the ways we describe a work of art that is sloppy or unfinished is as "a mess." The problem with lying, or lying by omission, is that it leaves everything incomplete—in a mess. Truth always completes the picture—any picture. And when a picture is complete, whole and integrated, we see it as "beautiful". .... Truth and beauty become impossible to separate.
>
> Truth leads you to a more confident level in your relationships with others and yourself. It diminishes fear and increases your sense of personal mastery. Lies and half-truths will always weigh you down, whereas truth

will clear up your thinking and give you the energy and clarity needed for self-motivation.

There are definitely rewards for integrity. In *The Book on Mind Management*, Dennis R. Deaton says, "Integrity is golden. Literally and figuratively more precious than rubies, we attain it as we seek it. Developing integrity, the portal to personal empowerment, happens incrementally, a step at a time. Yet the moment you make a strong commitment to strive for it, you acquire power! What counts most is your commitment to improve on this principle."

When we make a commitment to personal integrity, the Universe works in our favor. This was recognized by German philosopher Goethe when he said, "[The] moment one definitely commits oneself, then Providence moves, too. All sorts of things occur to help one that would never otherwise have occurred. A whole stream of events issues from the decision, raising in one's favor all manner of unforeseen incidents and meetings and material assistance, which no [woman] could have dreamed could come [her] way."

The following exercise will help you to work on and increase your personal integrity:

1. Make a list of the ways that your life is currently "in integrity."

Pat yourself on the back, as you are on your way to success as you strengthen your personal integrity.

2. Make a list of the ways that you are not now "in integrity."

In addition to thinking about honesty, ask yourself the following questions:

- Do I pay my bills on time?
- Do I do what I say I will do? (For example, if you tell someone that you will call, do you make that call?)
- Do I meet my time commitments?
- Do I make promises that are impossible to keep?
- Do I say what I think people want to hear, rather than speaking the truth? (Consider that sometimes it is better to say

nothing at all than to say something that is not true or to make an offensive comment.)

- Do I try to "look good" or cover up a mistake, rather than admitting the truth?
- Am I true to myself and who I am? Do I know who I am?
- Do I live my own values?

Ask yourself some of the following more specific questions:

- Am I working at the right job for me?
- Am I associating with people who are uplifting and positive?
- Do I live in the geographical area that is right for me?
- Do I live in fear or debt?
- Do I represent myself honestly?
- Do I put myself at undue physical risk?
- Do I take care of my health?
- Am I addicted to substances or compulsive behavior?

3. Analyze the source of each item on your list from number "2."

If these items are important to you, be sure to resolve all of them before moving to the next step. You might start by listing the consequences that result from each of them. Then write the changes you would need to make in order to eliminate the consequences and bring integrity to these parts of your life. It will help in your analysis if you also include anything that you may need to give up in order to bring these areas of your life into integrity.

4. Make a commitment to start living a life of integrity, as you define it.

Your integrity is unique to you, and you are the one who will decide what it means for you. You need to commit to commitment.

5. Let go of at least ten "shoulds," "coulds," "oughts," and "wills."

Most women were conditioned when they were little girls to try to be everything to everyone. As we grew up, we learned that this is impossible; however, we continue to try to do this by telling ourselves that we "should" do this or that or by making commitments that are impossible to keep.

6. Involve a coach or another strong person to help you.

Find an individual who is interested in partnering with you to help you to improve your personal integrity. This should be someone who truly cares about your well-being, wants the best for you, and is willing to tell you not only the things you want to hear.

7. Stop spending time with people who are not the best role models.

You know who these people are. Concentrate on spending your time with those people who are uplifting and from whom you receive the gift of positive energy.

8. Develop a realistic action plan for improving your personal integrity.

Keep this action plan simple. Include elements that you can actually do, rather than things that might occur. Once you have developed this plan, add it to your priority list, your goals, and your overall action plan that you developed earlier. Since personal integrity is a predecessor of success, I assume that it will be a priority for every woman who wants to create success in her life.

——— —— ——

Personal integrity is a personal choice. Either you want it for your life, or you don't. However, the benefits of living in integrity are numerous. As a woman increases her level of integrity, she begins to become aware of the following in her life:

- She has more energy.
- She feels effortlessness about achieving the desired results.
- She feels much less stress in her life.
- She attracts into her life more fulfilling people who are consistently reliable, empowering, loving, and inspiring.
- She enjoys a richer and more successful life.

In *Golden Nuggets*, Sir John Templeton says, "Probably the greatest secret to peace of mind is living the life of personal integrity—not what people think of you, but what you know of yourself. If you remain true to your ethical principles, your personal integrity can become an attractive beacon for success on every level. Listen carefully to the inner promptings of conscience and live peacefully."

Personal integrity is of utmost importance to success. It is your personal foundation on which you can build the woman you want to be.

CHAPTER

Enjoy the Moment!

Creating balance in your life

Paula is a wonderful planner. Each time I talk with her, she has had a "great brainstorm" for the next outing or social event. She plans fabulous parties, unique golf tournaments, adventuresome hiking trips, and unusual vacations. Everyone who participates in Paula's events tends to have a fantastic time. The only one who does not enjoy the events is Paula. Her lack of enjoyment stems from the fact that she is continually focusing on planning the next event, rather than the one that is occurring at the present time.

Now in her late-forties, Paula is still physically attractive. She is single and says that she would like to be married. Fifteen years ago, she told me that she wanted to have two children when she "found the right man and settled down." She has many dates, but rarely will she date a man a second time. She says she is looking for "Mr. Right" and even enlists some of her dates to help her look.

Paula is a unique woman. She has told me that she feels that life is passing her by as she dreams about and plans the future. She is not happy with her life and does not understand why this is so.

--- --- ---

Barbara is focused on her career. She is the first one to arrive at the office in the morning and the last one to leave in the evening, taking work home with her every night. She works at least seventy hours per week and has been promoted five times in six years. Her boss knows that he can depend on her to deliver results, even on very short notice.

Barbara, who is divorced and has two grown children living in another state, wishes she had more time to do something other than work. She would like to visit her children, but she doesn't want to take the time away from work. In fact, she has not taken a vacation for several years. Her friends no longer invite her to their get-togethers, because they know that she will again tell them that she has to work. She is constantly tired and does not understand the reason for this. She thinks maybe she should see a doctor, but she is having difficulty scheduling this into her workload. She says, "I wish the doctor's office was open at 2:00 A.M. when I am having trouble sleeping."

Barbara tells herself that, after her next promotion, she will take time to do the things she wants to do. This is the same thing she had said before her last promotion and the one before that.

--- --- ---

The stories of Paula and Barbara might look like extreme examples, but they are true. It is so easy for a woman to become absorbed in one part of her life and to get out of balance. We are meant to enjoy life. When we allow ourselves to be out of balance, we become more stressed and we enjoy life less. This limits our success.

Stopping to "smell the roses" is more than a cliché. It points out the importance of appreciating beauty, human relationships, and the things that are most important to us. It offers the opportunity to reflect, to decrease stress, and to add balance to our lives. This not only contributes to, but also enhances any success we may achieve.

When I received the job offer for my European assignment, both my husband, Cliff, and I were excited about the opportunity ahead of us. I developed goals and objectives for the European job long before we left the United States. I wanted to make sure that my accomplishments were significant for the two years that I would be there and didn't give much thought to the wonderful adventures that would be available.

After I had been in Europe for two weeks, I sent status reports through electronic mail to those who had been instrumental in helping me to receive the job offer. I will always cherish the answer that came from my United States human resource manager. He started by complimenting me on what I had already accomplished in the two weeks that I had been in Europe. He then added some advice by saying, "You will be given a lot of vacation time while you are on your European assignment. Be sure you take this time, and make it a point to see as much of Europe as you can. There are too many people who return from foreign assignments, never having taken advantage of the opportunity to explore the areas where they have lived. Many will remark, 'I worked so hard that I missed the party.' Enjoy the party while you are there."

I am grateful that this advice came very early during my European assignment. It allowed me to rethink my priorities and make the adjustments necessary to "enjoy the party" while still making the significant impact that I had planned. In fact, I think that the reason I was able to exceed my job objectives was due in part to the enjoyment of the adventures I experienced. Since Cliff was retired, he was able to travel with me on many of my business trips. I would plan meetings in London for Fridays and Mondays, so that we would be there for the weekend to spend time with friends, visit museums, and go to the theater. When we weren't in London or sightseeing in France, we would take short weekend trips to Germany, the Netherlands, and Belgium. We cruised the Mediterranean and Black Seas and took vacations in Italy, Spain, and Portugal. We also entertained many friends who visited us in France, and we enjoyed every minute. The added bonus was that I was able to exceed my objectives for the job assignment and to enjoy it even more than I had anticipated.

Many of the interviewees for this book say that they have been accused of spending their entire life working in order to reach the positions that they have held. However, this is not true. Although they focus on their careers, they also focus on their other priorities in life. They take time for themselves and for their families and friends. They truly enjoy life.

Dr. Bobbie Stevens, Unlimited Futures president, says, "It is so important to live in the *now*. The *now* is the one thing we can be sure of experiencing. Someone once said, 'Life is what happens when you are planning for your future.'"

Beth MacDonald, while Johnson & Johnson Asia/Pacific regional franchise director, said, "Taking time to enjoy the moment definitely reduces anxiety. For me, it also creates the time when the highest levels of performance take place. It is dancing without dancing, kind of a Zen state. It is critical to success."

Admittedly, it is difficult for women who are focused on their careers to consciously take the time to "smell the roses." One woman said, "I often feel that when I'm old and look back on my life, my main regret will be that I didn't enjoy the moment while I was living it. It won't be that I didn't achieve something, that I didn't make money, or that I didn't have the material things I wanted. I'm afraid that I won't feel that I have enjoyed it enough. My New Year's resolution this year was that, every time I went on a business trip, I was going to do one thing to have fun at my destination. It's hard to take the time to do it, but I'm doing it. There is something interesting to do on every business trip. I am taking the time, and I'm enjoying it."

Are you taking time to enjoy the moment and bring pleasure into your life? You might start by answering the following questions:

- Do I regularly take time for myself?
- Do I enjoy the company of special people?
- Do I enjoy the social events I attend?
- Do I live my priorities?
- Is my work challenging and fulfilling?

- Do I engage in recreational activities?
- Do I have at least one hobby?
- Do I take care of my health and have regular checkups?
- Do I exercise regularly?
- Do I give to others?
- Am I a grateful receiver?
- Do I have a way to relax that eliminates stress?
- Do I feel energized at the end of most work days?

If you have answered "yes" to all of these questions, congratulations! Otherwise, the following suggestions may be of help:

1. Be in the present.

My department was responsible for developing a comprehensive strategic plan for 3M's e-business, and top management had given us an extremely tight time line for delivering this plan. Several of the managers who reported to me worked long hours in order to meet the delivery schedule for the plan. At each critical point along the time line, we would meet to review progress and make any necessary modifications.

Late one Friday afternoon, one of the employees came to my office to ask when I would be leaving that day. She wanted to make sure that she gave me the latest draft of the plan to review that evening, so that I could get my recommendations back to her on Saturday morning. Her face was flushed from the intensity of the work that afternoon, and I was immediately concerned about her health. Mostly because of my concern for her, I explained that it was not necessary for her to get the draft to me that day. My husband and I had tickets for a professional football game that evening, and I would not have a chance to review the draft until Saturday morning. In her eagerness to meet the deadline, she replied, "I'll get it to you anyway." Half jokingly, she added, "So you can read it at the game!"

I brought the draft of the plan with me to the game and read it between plays. During plays, I thought about the future of e-business and the things that my department needed to accomplish in order to be successful in this emerging channel. I definitely was not living in the present, and I was not taking the time to enjoy the game. In fact, I didn't even know the score throughout most of it. In addition, I did not adequately review the plan document. In retrospect, I knew that it would have been much better for me to go to the game, enjoy the evening with my husband, and review the document the next morning when I could give it my full attention.

A colleague once said, "Being fully in the *present* is a *gift*. It is a gift to yourself as well as to others. You literally create your future with your thoughts and actions. When you are fully in the present, you are totally involved and alert to opportunities. The people you encounter subjectively sense whether or not you are fully with them. This has a great impact on the quality of your personal and business relationships."

2. Enjoy your work.

Nancy Albertini, chief executive officer of the executive search firm Taylor Winfield, says, "If you don't love what you do, don't do it. Successful people love what they do."

Are you working at a job that you love? If not, is there any possibility that you can make a change? A change does not necessarily mean a totally different job. It could mean adding or subtracting something from your current job in order to make it more enjoyable.

When I was in my early twenties, I observed that people's productivity on the job seemed to increase in correlation to how much they liked their jobs. I also found it much more pleasurable to work with those who enjoyed what they were doing. I resolved that, if I were ever in a position where I didn't enjoy my job, I would change jobs. Little did I know that my opportunity to do this would be just a few years later.

At the time, I was a systems analyst and had two children, a six-year-old boy and a six-month-old baby girl. I enjoyed my job, and I enjoyed my children even more. It seemed I had the best of both worlds when I was offered a promotion to a senior analyst position in another department. I accepted the new position because it was a promotion, not because the systems work would be more interesting. I soon realized that I had made a mistake. The work was boring and tedious, and there was not enough of it for the number of analysts hired to do it. As the days passed slowly, I thought about how nice it would be if I didn't have to work. I even daydreamed about catching up on my ironing. At that point, I realized the extent of my boredom.

I knew that I needed to make a change and that, because of my family finances, staying home was not an alternative. I could have returned to my previous job, but I was too proud to admit that I had made a mistake. I asked my boss for additional assignments, hoping for more of a challenge on my existing job. There was no additional work available for the department. As a result, I initiated an intensive job search, which culminated with my acceptance of a position at 3M.

Wayne Dyer, author of *Your Erroneous Zones* and *You'll See It When You Believe It,* says, "There is no scarcity of opportunity to make a living at what you love; there is only a scarcity of resolve to make it happen."

3. Take time for yourself.

Most women will take the time to nurture others, but few will take the time to nurture themselves. Although they know it intellectually, they do not always accept the fact that they can best help others when they are physically, emotionally, mentally, and spiritually healthy.

In *Take Time for Your Life*, personal coach Cheryl Richardson suggests that her readers give themselves permission to make the quality of their lives their top priority. She stresses this in the following excerpt from her book:

> A high-quality life starts with a high quality you. My basic coaching philosophy in working with clients is one of extreme self-care—the foundation of a rich and fulfilling life. This means putting your self-care above

anything else—saying no unless it's absolute yes, choosing to spend your time and energy on things that bring you joy, and making decisions based on what you want instead of what others want. It's a challenging concept for most.

Making your self-care a priority can be scary, even offensive, at first. Yet, as you begin to filter your decisions through the lens of extreme self-care, you'll find that your nagging inner voice becomes a strong ally in helping you to make better choices. You'll leave work early to keep that dinner engagement with a friend, or you'll go out for a walk during lunch instead of working straight through. And, best of all, you'll discover that when you start practicing extreme self-care, a Divine force rallies behind you to support your decisions and will actually make your life easier.

Do you take time for yourself? When is the last time you went for a walk in the park and enjoyed nature? Enjoyed a bubble bath? Had lunch with a friend? Read a book? If you had an entire day to do something spontaneous, what would it be? Why not do it now?

4. Give to others.

Have you ever noticed how good you feel when you give to someone else? Some women wait to give until they can afford to buy an extravagant gift. This is not necessary, as it is usually the nonmaterial gifts that the receiver values most. This can be as simple as a smile or a compliment. It can be the simple gift of showing someone that you care by giving him or her your attention. It can be taking the time to tell someone that you appreciate him or her. Although these gifts do not cost anything, they can be the most precious to both the receiver and the giver.

In the following passage from *The Seven Spiritual Laws of Success*, Dr. Deepak Chopra talks about giving:

> When you meet someone, you can silently send them
> a blessing, wishing them happiness, joy, and laughter.
> This kind of silent giving is very powerful.

One of the things I was taught as a child and, which I taught my children also, is never to go to anyone's house without bringing something—never visit anyone without bringing them a gift. You may say, "How can I give to others when at the moment I don't have enough myself?" You can bring a flower. One flower. You can bring a note or a card which says something about your feelings for the person you're visiting. You can bring a compliment. You can bring a prayer. Make a decision to give wherever you go, to whomever you see.

5. Engage in recreational activities.

In *Your Money or Your Life*, Joe Dominguez and Vicki Robin note that the average North American works twenty percent more today than in 1973 and has thirty-two percent less free time per week. Many of the working women I know tend to rush through recreational activities, if they take the time to engage in them at all. However, it is these recreational activities that help to reduce stress and add to the fuel needed to accomplish our goals in life.

A recreational activity can be as simple as a walk outdoors. It can be a hobby, a visit with a friend, a sporting event, a massage, or a vacation. Actually, it can be anything that you enjoy doing outside of work, including just taking time to relax.

The word *recreation* contains the root word *create*, which means, "to cause to exist." By preceding this word with the prefix *re*, which means "again" or "anew," we are saying that we are causing a new existence of ourselves. We are refreshing our lives, both mentally and physically.

Make a list of the ways that you are refreshing your life. From this list, you can determine whether you need to add some recreational activities that will help you to reduce stress and become a renewed, refreshed woman.

6. Express and feel gratitude.

Part of expressing gratitude is becoming a gracious receiver. Many women think that they should always be the giver, rather than the receiver; hence they have difficulty in accepting that which is given to them. Many have told me that they think they are not worthy or deserving.

You were born deserving of good things. If you do not remember this, look at a newborn baby. Is this baby deserving of love and happiness? You are no less deserving than you were on the day you were born. If you have doubt concerning your worthiness, look at your baby picture and remind yourself of this. When something good happens to you, tell yourself, "I deserve this." Be a gracious receiver, and express gratitude for that which you have been given.

Dr. Deepak Chopra suggests that we gratefully receive all the gifts that life has to offer us. These gifts include gifts of nature, such as sunlight, the sounds of singing birds, spring showers, and the beauty of the first snow of winter. They also include gifts from others, both material and nonmaterial.

— — —

In *Golden Nuggets*, Sir John Templeton says, "In order to be happy, healthy, and stress free, it is important to believe in yourself and your individual right to happiness and health. Take time to be out of doors. The beauty of the earth can stimulate joy, thanksgiving, and healthy thoughts. Learn to laugh and to be silent. Love your children and play with your pets. Life is to be lived and enjoyed!"

In these days of instant communication through the Internet, we have many opportunities that did not exist during our earlier years. While participating in a recent teleclass (a class where all participants attend via telephone), I met Sara Arbel, an Israeli mother of three, who is a successful businesswoman. During our first class session, Sara and I discovered that, despite the cultural differences, we have much in common. We have communicated almost daily through electronic mail since our first class together. Through these electronic mail messages, I have developed much respect for Sara and the decisions she has made in her life.

After her stint in the Israeli army, a responsibility required of all Israeli citizens, Sara married an aspiring artist. In the early years of her marriage, she pursued a higher education with course work in behavioral science, communication, and consumer psychology. She and her husband then moved to Canada, where she established an art gallery to market her husband's works of art. The customers kept returning, and she and her husband received large commissions. After nearly a decade, the couple and their children returned to their native Israel where Sara next established two businesses, one specializing in corporate image design and the other in marketing consulting. One business supplied work to the other, and they both became financially lucrative. She headed these companies as she was also raising her children. As the children got older, she traveled the world with her customers, who were from various industries, including electronics, plastics, agriculture, textile, medicine, and others. She competed well and was respected by her competitors. Her major challenges were during times of war when the entire economy was shaken. Still, she was extremely successful in business.

It seemed that Sara was living the ideal life—a good husband and family, a successful career, world travel, and financial security. Then her husband died. As a result, she threw herself even more into her career, working fourteen to sixteen hours each day.

Ultimately, Sara came to the realization that life was more than work alone. She decided to decrease her number of work hours and to take time for her life. She is successful in her current profession as a consultant and a personal and professional coach. She is also successful in all other facets of her life.

When I asked Sara what she considers to be the greatest success in her life so far, she replied, "The greatest success in my life so far is arriving at the realization that, at this stage of my life, I cannot define such a thing as 'greatest success.' For there are so many aspects of our complex lives that need attending. Career is just one of them. What about the other aspects? Am I my career? Am I my profession? Am I my relationship with a spouse, children, friends, and community? Is success in all these areas reflecting on my being a success? And what about me? Am I evolving, growing, expanding, and leading a balanced life where my love of myself is being attended?"

When asked what advice she would give to women who want to achieve success in their lives, Sara said, "Don't forget yourself in the process of building a successful career. Forgetting yourself through this process is not a success in your life, but a success in only one aspect of your life. It may be an aspect that fills your life with a sense of fullness, but it is the fullness of a fool, for the grave-yard is full of people who thought they were irreplaceable. Don't mistake between the making of a living and the making of a life, as the making of a life is the most valuable success story where you will leave a mark in the world. Your career will always be someone else's better craftsmanship. Invest first in yourself. . . .The rest will follow."

In *Tuesdays with Morrie*, Mitch Albom interviewed Morrie Schwartz, who was dying of amyotrophic lateral sclerosis, or what is more commonly known as Lou Gehrig's Disease. Mitch asked Morrie what he would do if he had one perfectly healthy day. Morrie gave the following reply:

> I would get up in the morning, do my exercises, have a lovely breakfast of sweet rolls and tea, go for a swim, then have my friends over for a nice lunch. I'd have them come one or two at a time so we could talk about their families, their issues, talk about how much we mean to each other.
>
> Then I'd go for a walk in a garden with some trees, watch their colors, watch the birds, take in the nature that I haven't seen in so long now.
>
> In the evening, we'd all go together to a restaurant with some great pasta, maybe some duck—I love duck—and then we'd dance the rest of the night. I'd dance with all the wonderful dance partners out there, until I was exhausted. And then I'd go home and have a deep, wonderful sleep.

Mitch was surprised by Morrie's answer. He expected Morrie to say that, on his perfect day, he would fly to Italy or have lunch with the president. Instead, Morrie's answer was simple. It seemed average. During his illness, Morrie had had much time to reflect on life and the things that brought him pleasure. It is sometimes the simplest things that bring us the most pleasure.

— — —

Often, when a woman is diagnosed with a terminal illness, she begins to think about what she would have done differently in her life. She thinks about her priorities and how she has lived.

If you knew that you had just six more months to live and that you would have your health during this time, how would you live your life? What would you do differently? In contemplating these questions, I made a list of the things I would do.

- I would spend more time with my family and friends.
- I would be more spontaneous.
- I would show more emotions, laugh more, smile more and cry more in front of other people.
- I would take better care of my body through exercise, sleep and nutrition.
- I would not be concerned about what others think of me, but about what I think of myself.
- I would record messages about life for my grandchildren, Alea and Ethan, and those who are still to be born.
- I would make myself more available to those in need and those less fortunate than I.
- I would spend less time talking and more time listening.
- I would look for opportunities to engage in anonymous acts of kindness, even for people I do not know.
- I would open my eyes to the beauty of nature and enjoy witnessing the miracle of creation.
- I would express my love for other people, both in my words and in my actions.

After making this list, I decided that I didn't have to wait to do these things until I have just six months left of my life. I can do them now.

Take time now to make your list. Then seize the joy of the day, savor each moment as special and appreciate the beauty of life.

CHAPTER

Continue to Learn!

Engaging in lifelong learning

Just as my MBA degree opened doors for me before I had gained the experience needed for a particular position, education has been an important factor for many women searching for expanded opportunities in the business world. Almost all of the women I interviewed have college degrees. Some have master's degrees, two have doctorates, and one is a medical doctor.

While a few of my interviewees do not have college educations, they nonetheless are enjoying success in their lives. One reason for their success is that they are committed to the other nine strategies for success. Just as the women with degrees, they are committed to a lifelong learning program. Each and every one of these successful women stresses the importance of a continuing process of learning.

It is easy to procrastinate the development of a learning plan, especially for those who are living a hurry-up lifestyle. However, no matter how hectic your life is, you will become more successful if you make time to continue your learning. Following are some of the options for incorporating learning into your life:

1. Obtain a formal education.

Nineteenth century biologist Thomas Huxley said, "Perhaps the most valuable result of all education is the ability to make yourself do the thing you have to do when it ought to be done, whether you like it or not. It is the first lesson that [should] be learned and however early a person's training begins, it is probably the last lesson a person learns thoroughly."

In addition to being an excellent opportunity to learn, formal education opens doors. If your work experience is limited, a formal education is a way to let a prospective employer know that you can persevere, meet objectives, and succeed.

If you are interested in a particular profession, chances are you will need an education in the associated subject matter in order to enter that profession. When I decided to be a computer programmer in the 1960s, computers were still new, and related college curriculums did not yet exist. I followed the path of my uncle, who had majored in mathematics and was working as a computer programmer. Because of my marriage at age nineteen and the resulting family financial situation, my full-time education was cut short after one year of college. I continued my education by taking college classes at night in mathematics, statistics, and computer programming. I later added business courses and changed my major to business management. It took me until I was thirty years old to earn my bachelor's degree, but I did it!

I later earned my MBA degree in the same way—by attending classes at night while working full time during the day. This is not the easiest way to obtain a college education, but many successful women (and men) have done it this way. Since obtaining a college education is time consuming, it is important to examine one's priorities before engaging in a degree program while working full time. If you decide to do this, start by evaluating the many alternatives now available for class participation. These include video classes, teleclasses and Internet classes, in addition to the traditional classroom setting.

2. Attend seminars and workshops.

Each day, thousands of seminars, workshops, and conferences are offered in various locations throughout the United States. Many of these are related to particular professions, and others provide personal growth and development. Some of them are free of charge, such as workshops offered by some church groups and nonprofit organizations.

Be selective when determining which seminars, workshops, and conferences to attend. Because of the number of these types of learning opportunities available, make sure that the ones you attend are the ones that will be the most beneficial, either professionally or personally.

Most people retain very little of what they learn in a typical seminar or workshop. For this reason, I recommend that you take notes on those topics that are the most relevant to you. Be sure to review these notes before much time has elapsed. During your review, develop an action plan on how you will apply what you have learned. If this action plan contains even one item that will be of benefit for you, it was worth the time you invested in attending the seminar.

3. Read books, magazines, newspapers, and information available on the Internet.

A wealth of information on myriad subjects is available in print and via the Internet. One of the great things about learning from these sources is that you can engage in this type of learning from almost anyplace, including in the comfort of your own home.

My advice in selecting reading material is the same as that for selecting conferences and workshops. Because of the quantity of books, magazines, and newspapers available, we need to be selective. This applies to the reading that we do for enjoyment, as well as the reading that we do in order to learn. It is unrealistic and counterproductive to attempt to read everything that comes into your home or office. Attempting to do so becomes overwhelming and can cause you to neglect your priorities.

Read good books and other information. Determine which reading material is best for you by monitoring your attention span as you are reading, determining how much of the material you retain, and evaluating your feelings after reading the material. You will then improve your ability to select better reading material in the future.

4. Enhance your listening skills.

Listening to the spoken word is another way that we can learn. By staying alert and listening to that which is happening around us, we learn so much more than we do when we are speaking. A mother learns to identify her baby's needs by listening to his different cries. A child learns to stay away from danger by listening to his or her mother's warnings. A factory worker learns to properly perform her job responsibilities by listening to her foreperson's instructions. We all learn by listening to those who know more about a subject than we do.

In *The Art of Managing People*, authors Phillip L. Hunsaker and Anthony J. Alessandra offer the following tips for "power listening":

- Don't interrupt.
- Listen for main ideas.
- Concentrate on substance, not style.
- Fight distractions.
- Stifle anger.
- Take brief notes.
- Let others talk first.
- Empathize.
- Withhold judgment.
- React to the message.
- Read the feelings between the lines.
- Ask questions.

By spending more time listening and less time talking, we create learning opportunities that will increase our effectiveness and, ultimately, our success.

5. Listen to audiotapes.

We are living in a time of convenience with the many classes, seminars, and books that are available on audiotape. If you have a tape player in your car, you are able to make your driving time more productive by listening to tapes. If you cannot afford to buy audiotapes, you can check them out at your local library or exchange tapes with others. Many companies also have libraries or human resource departments, which will lend learning tapes to employees.

If your only venue for listening to audiotapes is your car, it is advisable to listen to the tapes several times to maximize your learning opportunity. Some speakers recommend that you listen to a tape five or six times. However, if you listen to a tape for the first time while driving, you might want to also make time available to listen to it a second time when you can give it your full attention and take notes. You can then use these notes as you develop your learning plan.

6. Learn from life's experiences.

When my daughter was a teenager, I felt that I was constantly protecting and correcting her. When I realized that she resented this, I told her that I had made many mistakes in my life and that I would like to help her to learn from my mistakes. I thought that this would protect her from experiencing some of the pain I had felt as a result of these mistakes. Her answer surprised me when she said, "Mom, don't you think I will learn more from my own mistakes than I will learn from yours?" As much as I disliked the idea of my child experiencing pain, I realized she was right. We can learn from the experiences of others, but we learn even more from our own experiences, both positive and negative.

Successful women tend to be extremely aware of what is happening around them. They learn from both their own and other people's experiences. The things, which many people would call failures, are not failures to these women. They are learning opportunities. One of these women failed her first test in graduate school. She said, "This showed me that I needed to work harder and to be more committed to what I was doing." She is convinced that her initial failure served as an inspiration to succeed.

One successful woman was terminated from one of her positions. She told me that this was a great learning opportunity, because it helped her realize what she needed to do to improve her style. It also made her a stronger person. Since that time, she has excelled in every position she has held.

Each of us has hundreds of experiences from which we can learn each day. We learn through awareness, observation, and participation. Most of these learning opportunities have no financial cost to us, and they can provide substantial benefit to us.

In *Golden Nuggets*, Sir John Templeton says, "Wherever we are and whatever we are doing, it is possible to learn something that can enrich our lives and the lives of others. . . . No one's education is ever complete."

7. Challenge yourself with new experiences.

When Connie Carroll had been married for twenty-five years, she knew that she was a good wife, mother, grandmother, and homemaker. However, she wanted to increase her self-confidence, and she resolved to do this by overcoming her two major fears in life— speaking in public and swimming. To demonstrate her commitment, she entered the Mrs. Minnesota pageant as one of the few grandmothers to compete in this competition.

Connie had had a lifelong fear of water. Since she would be required to model aerobic wear during the pageant, she engaged in an exercise program to become more physically fit and to lose some weight. She chose swimming as one of her main exercises and embarked on a rigorous routine of lessons and practice. She swam three or four times each week. She not only lost weight and became more physically fit, but she also learned to be a good swimmer and overcame her fear of water.

Connie's next challenge was learning to be comfortable when speaking in public. This was a difficult one, as it is for most people. In fact, it is the number one fear of people in general. She knew that, during the pageant, she would be interviewed by judges and would also speak to the audience from the stage. She worked with a coach and then put what she learned into practice by extensive role-playing of mock interviews with family and friends. She became more comfortable speaking in public and eventually spoke not only at the pageant but also on television. "From this experience, I feel that I have become much more confident in myself and a more positive person" she told me. "I have learned that I have the ability to achieve the things I want. I have also learned how I can improve the way I communicate with others and the way I present myself."

Connie has since participated in three Mrs. Minnesota pageants, and she considers each of them a learning experience. She has enjoyed each pageant and has won awards for her community involvement and for having the best "pitch book." Her pitch book contains family pictures, certificates for volunteer work, diplomas, ribbons from dog shows, poems she had written, samples of her photography, and information on the ways she has represented her county. Preparing and using it enabled her to highlight areas in which she already had achieved a degree of success, and it was a great resource when she set out to solicit companies and individuals to sponsor her in the pageant.

Connie considers it a great honor to have been recognized for her community involvement. "This is an area that is so important to me and about which I feel so strongly. Being involved in organizations in your area shows you care about what is happening in your city, county, and schools. When you are aware, you can help to make positive changes."

Connie's community involvement has also provided learning experiences for her. Her volunteer activities in her school district, city, and state have helped more than thirty organizations. In her most recent volunteer activity, she is helping disabled people to ride horses. She explained, "Because of the motion of the horse, this program provides a therapeutic experience for disabled persons. It rhythmically moves the rider's body in a manner similar to a human walk. Physically disabled riders can show improvement in flexibility, balance, and muscle strength. The unique relationship formed with the horse can lead to increased confidence, patience, and self-esteem for people with mental or emotional disabilities."

Connie Carroll is a successful woman who has challenged herself and stepped out of her comfort zone in order to learn and to grow. Each of us has the opportunity to learn by challenging ourselves with new experiences. Start by making a list of areas in your life that you want to strengthen. From this, you can do some brainstorming regarding the things you might do in order to develop the strength you desire. Engaging in such a plan itself requires strength, but, as Connie has demonstrated, it is indeed achievable.

8. Work with a personal and/or professional coach or mentor.

Of the women interviewed, only two had ever had a formal mentor; however, most of them were able to cite people who had been informal mentors to them during their careers. All of these women paid tribute to these mentors as significant contributors to their success.

There are thousands of professional coaches available to assist individuals in learning how to create success in their lives. According to Thomas Leonard, founder of Coach University, people hire coaches for the following reasons:

- To set better goals.
- To reach their goals faster.
- To make significant changes.
- To become more financially successful.
- To design—and live—the perfect life.
- To get ahead professionally.
- To make better decisions.
- To have someone with whom to collaborate.
- To improve their relationships.
- To make a bigger impact on the world.
- To simplify their life.
- To strengthen their personal foundation.

- To reduce stress and tolerations (unwanted things that they put up with).
- To increase income or revenues.
- To become a better manager, executive, or businessperson.

A coach or a mentor can be a valuable asset to you as you develop your learning plan and take action to create success in your life.

9. Develop a personal learning plan.

Do you have a personal learning plan? If not, you are not alone, as most people do not take the time to develop such plans. As a result, many people participate in learning activities that do not align with their top priorities and goals.

A personal learning plan need not be elaborate, nor does it need to take a long time to develop. Start by reviewing your priorities and goals and determining what it is that you need to know in order to achieve what you want in life. From there, you can decide the best methods for learning that which you need and/or want to know. By using the tips in this chapter, you can make a chronological list of your plans for acquiring the learning you want and need. It can be as simple as that. Why not take the time now to develop this plan?

When she was Johnson & Johnson Asia/Pacific regional franchise director, Beth MacDonald believed in the importance of continuous learning plans for both herself and her employees. She ensured that her employees participated in team training, technical training, self-awareness training, leadership training and management training. As a result, she and her employees were able to lead and participate in high-performance teams that continually exceeded expectations.

Continuous, lifelong learning is important to success. Albert Einstein once said, "Education is that which remains when one has forgotten everything he learned in school." That which you learn throughout life contributes to your education and to your success.

CHAPTER

Increase Your Success!

Creating an ideal life for yourself

What does success look like to you? For most women, this is a difficult question. We might point to another woman and say that she is successful; however, we may be judging success by observing only one dimension of this woman's life. In selecting interview candidates for this book, my first criterion was that a woman needed to be successful in her own eyes and her own mind.

Most of the women I interviewed are businesswomen holding positions that have typically been labeled as men's jobs. Each of them has attained success, but they agree that a successful career is not the only component of a successful life. All feel they would have been successful in any career they might have chosen, whether that career was stereotyped as that of a man or that of a woman.

You can determine what success means to you personally. It might include a well-paying career, a job that pays less but is emotionally or spiritually rewarding, or a job that you leave behind when you go home from work, but pays well enough to buy the things you want and need. It can also mean being a full-time homemaker. The bottom line is that only you can define your own success.

Betty Notto, who you met briefly at the end of Chapter 3, is one of the most successful women I know. The ninth of eleven children in her family, she was born shortly before the Great Depression. Although the family did not have a great deal of money, they had the things they needed. They were a close family, and the ones who are still living continue to be close.

Betty married her high school sweetheart, Len Notto, while they were both still in high school. They had six children, two of them while Betty and Len were still teenagers. Len worked sixteen-hour-days to support the family, and Betty stayed home to care for their family. She took care of the house and the garden. In addition to all the basic household chores, she sewed clothing for the children, darned socks, canned pickles, and made homemade jelly. She has now been a full-time homemaker for more than fifty-five years.

When I asked Betty for her personal definition of success, she replied, "To me, success is not earning a lot of money or having a lot of worldly possessions. It's relationships, family, and friendships. If I've been a good wife, a good mother, and a good friend through the years, I feel I've been successful."

In retrospect, Betty admits that she has not always felt successful. She says she was more materialistic when she was younger. As she matured, she says she found that the material things were not as important to her as were the people she has touched, the people she loves, and the people who love her. The turning point came after she had been married for about twenty-nine years, when she and her husband attended a marriage enrichment program called Marriage Encounter. As a part of the program, the participants were asked to make a list of what they like about themselves. "I really had to think about what qualities I had in me that I liked," she said. "And, by golly, I came up with some, and that started to change my life!" She learned that she had many strengths and talents that she could use to enrich not only her life but also the lives of her family and others. She resolved to use these talents and strengths more fully to make people's lives better.

Betty and Len became active in Marriage Encounter and were recently honored for the many contributions they have made to this program over the past twenty-five years. Betty says that her participation in this program has helped her to realize her self worth and to enable her to make a positive difference in the lives of other people.

Betty has given of herself in many ways to make a difference in the lives of others. When her children were young, she was involved in the school parent/teacher organizations, Cub Scouts, Boy Scouts, Girl Scouts, and 4-H Club. Since her children have grown, she has been a leader in numerous other volunteer activities, which have enriched the lives of thousands of people.

Betty and Len both are indeed special to the people they have met. Their volunteer work has been featured in magazines, newspaper articles, and radio tributes. They often receive letters from people they have touched through Marriage Encounter and other volunteer activities. The following is from Jeffrey C. Wehe, who attended a Marriage Encounter weekend with his wife, Beverly.

> Beverly and I felt so strongly about this past weekend's experience and your leadership that we want to make sure it is memorialized in this letter. . . . The weekend was not as we had expected. The materials, presentations, format, location, and time frame were very effective.
>
> More importantly, we wanted to express our impressions of you, Betty and Len. In my lifetime, I can count on one hand those people who have touched me deeply. You are among those people. Although our time spent together was brief and our personal discussion and interaction limited, you strongly impressed us. Your powerful character, rock solid faith, leadership, willingness to take personal risk, and wonderful humor were the catalysts to open and honest communication. You both have tremendous personalities, which make you a natural magnet and attract people to you. You are then able to use your talents to positively influence people.

> I would argue that age alone does not develop these qualities. You shared with us some of your vulnerabilities, weaknesses, and failures. You revealed that you are not immune to the "human condition." You both have a strong positive attitude. I also believe it is how you have reacted to your challenges that has made the difference.
>
> Thank you for being a powerful influence on us during our weekend.

Although Betty has made it a priority to enrich the lives of others, her top priorities in life have always been her husband, her children, her grandchildren, and her great-grandchildren. She has been a strong emotional support to Len in his businesses throughout the years. She is also a wonderful mother, grandmother, and great-grandmother. She is indeed a successful woman! I'm proud to say that Betty Notto is my mother.

When my parents celebrated their fiftieth wedding anniversary, their children planned a party for 300 guests. When the guests arrived, the caterer almost panicked when she saw the number of people who attended. The total count was 417! It seemed that so many people wanted to be part of this special occasion with Betty and Len that many of them came, even without a formal invitation. After the meal, the dance was shorter than planned because of the many people who wanted to give speeches to honor this special couple. Betty herself had written six speeches, one for each of her six children. Since I am the oldest, her first speech was for me:

> Joanie, I always loved you the most because you were our first child, our first miracle. You were the fulfillment of very young love, the promise of our infinity.
>
> You sustained your dad and me through some very lean years—our first apartment furnished in early poverty with other people's hand-me-downs.
>
> You were the most beautiful baby, a gift from God. You had dark eyes and a lot of dark hair. You were our

"original" model, the test pattern for unsure parents trying to work out the bugs of being a mommy and a daddy.

You had new clothes, boiled bottles, and warm undershirts. You even had one set of unused grandparents. You may have suffered a wee bit from our youth, inexperience, and over-protectiveness. But we gave you all that we had. We gave you our love.

You were so pretty and so smart. Grandpa Notto gave you math lessons long before you were old enough for school. Your Uncle Ralph introduced you to the computer when you were fourteen, and you decided on a career in that field.

You had a grandma who would wake you when she visited, just so she could hold you and rock you to sleep again.

You were our beginning.

We are very proud of the success you have experienced in your career. But, most of all, we are proud of the loving, caring person you have become. We wish you and Cliff happiness in your marriage.

We love you, and we thank God for you, Joanie.

When Betty read the first sentence, some people in the audience gasped. Was Betty choosing favorites among her children when she said she always loved me the most? The people in the audience received their answer when she read her second speech, which was to my brother Lenny. She started, "Lenny, I always loved you the most because. . . ." When she spoke to each of her six children, she told why she loved each of them the most.

The anniversary party was to be a tribute to her and my dad, but she turned it around to be a tribute to her children and to the guests. She is a woman who has made, and continues to make, a very positive mark among the people she has touched. She has defined success for herself and is living a successful life.

How do you personally define success? If you could create the ideal life for yourself, what would that be? If you don't have your own definition, it might help to review the definitions given by some of the interviewees in the introduction:

- Success is a mental, physical, emotional, and spiritual balance in one's life.
- Success is being who one wants to be and doing what one wants to do.
- Success is feeling good about oneself.
- Success is making a contribution in this life and leaving a legacy for which one can be proud.
- Success is being able to fulfill our desires in all areas of life.
- Success is being able to determine one's own direction and to set one's own limits.
- Success is being able to do what God gave one the talents to do, based on what one has experienced and the lessons learned in doing so.

Once you have defined what success means to you, you are in a position to achieve that success. If you have completed the exercises in this book, you are on the road to increasing your success. You first need to believe in yourself.

When I was fourteen years old, my goal was to be a computer programmer, even though this was not a common field of endeavor for women at that time. I believed that I could do it and, although I took some detours along the way, I did become a computer programmer. Later, after I had designed computer systems for marketing and sales, I decided that I wanted to combine my computer experience with marketing to enhance the effectiveness of marketing and sales. This led to the management of functions that did not exist before I became involved in them. All along, I knew that I could do it. And I did!

Once you have defined what success looks like for you, the next step is to visualize that success. Remember to visualize the result of this success as if it has already happened.

Be aware of your priorities in life, and set your goals and act according to these priorities. Be sure that your priorities are aligned with your values and your definition of success. The more you act according to your priorities, the more likely it will be that you will enjoy success.

Take time to focus on those things that are most important to you. You may need to practice the focusing exercises in order to increase your ability to focus.

Evaluate your attitude each day, and stay away from the three C's—complaining, criticizing, and condemning. The more positive your attitude, the more you will attract that which is positive into your life.

Personal integrity is tantamount to success. Before making a commitment, be sure you will keep it. Let your word be your bond.

Create balance in your life. Take time to be spontaneous and to have fun. We are meant to enjoy life.

Take advantage of every opportunity to learn. Before going to bed each night, think about the things that you have learned that day and the ways that you will apply these things in creating your ideal life and in enriching the lives of others.

> A successful life involves personal relationships, family experiences, and spiritual involvement, as well as our professional lives. There may be many life possibilities for each of us. Success is finding out which of these may be the most meaningful, working hard for these dreams, and giving credit for the help and guidance necessary to fulfill them.
>
> —Sir John Templeton

By integrating and incorporating the ten success strategies into your life, you will increase your potential for enjoying the success that you seek. The ten success strategies really work! They have worked for me, for the book interviewees, and for the women that I have coached and mentored. They will work for you, too. I wish you success!

Appendix A

Reference Guide

To Creating Success in Your Life

Individual Definitions/Components of Success
- Mental, physical, emotional, and spiritual balance in one's life
- Being who one wants to be and doing what one wants to do
- Feeling good about oneself
- Making a contribution in this life and leaving a legacy for which one can be proud
- Fulfilling our desires in all areas of life
- Determining one's own direction and setting one's own limits
- Doing what God gave one the talents to do, based on what one has experienced and the lessons learned in doing so
- Whatever you define success to be for you

Strategies for Success
- Believe in Yourself!
- Dare to Dream!
- Determine Your Priorities!
- Set Powerful Goals!
- Ready—Aim—Take Action!
- Stay Focused!
- Remain Positive, No Matter What!
- Live your Life with Integrity!
- Enjoy the Moment!
- Continue to Learn!

Ways to Increase Self-esteem

- Think of yourself as the important person you are.
- Practice daily personal affirmations.
- Emulate self-confident people.
- Reward yourself for each success.
- Surround yourself with positive people.
- Look and feel your best.
- Fake it until you make it.
- Affirm those around you.

Relaxation Process

1. Sit down, close your eyes, and let the chair support your body.
2. Uncross your legs and feel yourself sink into the chair.
3. Take a deep breath, inhaling slowly. Hold your breath. Then slowly exhale as you imagine the tension leaving your body. Repeat this four times, each time becoming more aware of your breathing.
4. Let all your muscles relax as much as you can before going through the following steps.
5. Tense the muscles of your feet and ankles, curling your toes. Gently release this tension until your feet and ankles are totally relaxed.
6. Tense the muscles in the lower part of your legs. Slowly release this tension.
7. Tense the muscles in your upper legs. As before, slowly release the tension from your legs. Your legs, ankles, and feet should now be fully relaxed and feel like they are hanging limply.
8. Tense you hips and abdomen. As before, let this area of your body relax slowly.
9. Tense your chest and back muscles. Slowly, gently relax these muscles.
10. Direct your attention to your hands. Quickly make two fists, and slowly relax your hands.
11. Bend your wrists. Then relax them.
12. Tense the muscles in your lower arms. Slowly let them relax. Do the same with your upper arms.

13. Shrug your shoulders. Let them relax. Shrug them a second time, and then let them relax even more. Your arms are now beginning to hang comfortably by your sides.

14. Turn your head from side to side as far as it will go. Do this again. Touch your chin to your chest, and then raise it as high as you can. Relax your neck muscles.

15. Clench your teeth tightly together. Now relax your jaw muscles. Smile as broadly as you can. Then relax your mouth. Wrinkle your nose. Relax it. Close your eyes tighter. Relax them. Wrinkle your forehead. Relax it, feeling the tension flow out of your head.

16. If there still are any tense muscles in your body, direct your attention to these muscles. Relax them one-by-one.

Visualization Process

1. Determine what you want to create in your life.
2. Eliminate distractions.
3. Relax your body and your mind.
4. Create a mental movie.
5. Reinforce your vision through consistent mental rehearsal.

Steps to Setting Priorities

1. Determine your true values.
2. Prioritize your value list.
3. Plan and prioritize your activities.
4. Make time for your highest priorities.

Effective Delegation Tips

- Have confidence in the employee, and expect that he or she will do the task well.
- Treat the employee as you want others to treat you. Show the employee that you know that he or she will do the task well.
- As much as possible, match the project with the employee's skills and desires. Also, if possible, allow some leeway that will help the employee grow and develop in the job.
- Delegate the authority to accomplish a task along with the responsibility.

- Don't delegate projects or tasks that are impossible for the employee to do. Eliminate roadblocks along the way.
- Explain the assignment clearly. Ensure that the employee knows what is expected as far as results and timing.
- After delegating a project or task, get out of the employee's way. Make sure that the employee knows what is expected. Be available if he or she has questions or needs assistance.
- For longer projects, ask for periodic status reports. Make it clear that you need to be kept in the loop.
- Give the employees credit for the work that they do. Match the recognition with the project and the employee.

Setting Powerful Goals

- Commit your goals to paper.
- Assure that your goals are realistic and achievable, but give them some "stretch" to allow room for growth.
- Clearly define your goals.
- Visualize your goals as if you have already achieved them.
- Describe the benefits of your goals.
- Commit to accomplishing your goals.
- Develop and implement an action plan.

Additional Goal-setting Tips

- Identify your major obstacles to goal achievement.
- Set a deadline and a schedule for accomplishment.
- Reward yourself as you reach milestones on the way to accomplishing your goal.
- Review your goals every morning and every evening.
- Be clear about what you want to accomplish, but be flexible in between.

Decision Analysis Process

1. On a piece of paper, draw a chart showing the alternative decisions across the top and the decision-making criteria along the left side. Under each alternative, leave room for two columns that will be used later in this analysis. (See Appendix B.)
2. For each criterion, assign a weight between 1 and 5, and write this weight next to the criterion.

3. Evaluate each alternative for each criterion by assigning a score between 0 and 5, with "5" meaning the alternative very highly meets the criterion and "0" meaning that the alternative does not at all meet the criterion. Write the score in the cell (the box at the cross-section of the alternative and the criterion).
4. Multiply the weight of the criterion by the score of the criterion for each alternative. Write this number in a separate column under each alternative.
5. Add the weighted scores for each alternative.
6. Compare the totals. (If one of the totals is significantly higher than the others, this is the alternative that best meets the criteria. If there is not a significant difference between the highest total and the second highest total, you can either make a judgment call or add more criteria.)

Problem-solving Process

1. Write a synopsis of the current situation, clearly describing the problem. Be as objective as possible.
2. Determine the root cause of the problem. This might start with a list of probable causes. Take into consideration that the problem may be a symptom of another problem and that there can be more than one root cause.
3. Evaluate the root cause to determine what can be changed.
4. Brainstorm alternative solutions for solving the problem.
5. Evaluate each of the alternative solutions.
6. Select and implement the best alternative.

Handling Distractions

1. Set aside quiet time during the day to focus on your top priorities or action steps.
2. Decrease the stress in your body and your mind through relaxation.
3. Keep a piece of paper and a pen at hand while you are concentrating on a project or task. When an unrelated thought enters your mind, write it down.
4. Continue to record your distractions and the methods that you use to deal with them.

Methods for Improving Attitude
- Refrain from complaining, criticizing and condemning.
- Eliminate worry from your life.
- Put on a happy face.
- Look for the good in everything.
- Know that you can do it.
- Laugh.
- Value other people.
- Set an example.
- Give back to society.

Method for Enhancing Integrity
1. Make a list of the ways that your life is currently "in integrity."
2. Make a list of the ways that you are not now "in integrity."
3. Analyze the source of each item on your list from number "2."
4. Make a commitment to start living a life of integrity, as you define it.
5. Let go of at least ten "shoulds," "coulds," "oughts," and "wills."
6. Involve a coach or another strong person to help you.
7. Stop spending time with people who are not the best role models.
8. Develop a realistic action plan for improving your personal integrity.

Ways to Create Balance and Enjoy Life
- Be in the present.
- Enjoy your work.
- Take time for yourself.
- Give to others.
- Engage in recreational activities.
- Express and feel gratitude.

Options for Learning
- Obtain a formal education.
- Attend seminars and workshops.
- Read books, magazines, newspapers, and information available on the Internet.
- Enhance your listening skills.

- Listen to audiotapes.
- Learn from life's experiences.
- Challenge yourself with new experiences.
- Work with a personal and/or professional coach or mentor.
- Develop a personal learning plan.

Appendix B
Decision Analysis Chart

Criteria	Weight	Alternative 1		Alternative 2		Alternative 3		Alternative 4	
		Score	Weight x Score	Score	Weight x Score	Score	Weight x Score	Score	Weight x Score
Totals									

Appendix C

Recommended Reading

Albom, Mitch. *Tuesdays with Morrie*. New York, N.Y.: Doubleday, 1997.

Benton, Debra A. *Lions Don't Need to Roar*. New York, N.Y.: Warner Books, 1994

Chandler, Steve. *100 Ways to Motivate Yourself*. Franklin Lakes, N.J.: Career Press, 1996.

Chandler, Steve. *Reinventing Yourself*. Franklin Lakes, N.J.: Career Press, 1998.

Covey, Stephen R. *The 7 Habits of Highly Effective People*. New York, N.Y.: Simon & Schuster, 1990.

Deaton, Dennis R. *The Book on Mind Management*. Mesa, Ariz.: MMI Publishing, 1994.

Dyer, Wayne W. *You'll See It When You Believe It*. New York, N.Y.: Avon Books, 1990.

Maltz, Maxwell. *Psycho-Cybernetics*. New York, N.Y.: Pocketbooks, 1987.

Peale, Norman Vincent. *The Power of Positive Thinking*. Englewood Cliffs, N.J.: Prentice-Hall, Inc., 1987.

Richardson, Cheryl. *Take Time for Your Life*. New York, N.Y.: Broadway Books, 1999.

Stevens, Bobbie. *Unlimited Futures*. (To be published in 2001.)

Templeton, Sir John. *Golden Nuggets*. Radnor, Pa.: Templeton Foundation Press, 1997.

vos Savant, Marilyn. *Brain Building*. New York, N.Y.: Bantam Doubleday Dell Publishing, 1991.

Index

About the Author

Joan Eleanor Gustafson, founder and president of Success and Leadership Dynamics, has coached hundreds of individuals in achieving their desired results, both in their careers and in their personal lives. Her specialties include:

- Designing and structuring organizations to maximize results through optimal use of resources (people, money, tangible assets and materials)
- Individual growth and development
- Effective deployment of teams
- Professional and personal coaching
- Customizing and facilitating workshops on success and leadership

Prior to founding Success and Leadership Dynamics, Joan was a member of the Corporate Marketing Management Committee at 3M, where she held management positions for twenty-six years. Her management and leadership responsibility included the areas of e-business, marketing services, customer satisfaction, sales and marketing productivity improvement, sales support systems, information technology, sales rep training, knowledge transfer, communications services, and strategic outsourcing. Her international responsibility included a two-year assignment in Europe, where she lived in Paris, France.

Joan holds a B.A. degree in business management and an MBA in management. She has served on boards of directors of nonprofit organizations and is a member of the National Speakers Association, the American Society for Training and Development, and International Coach Federation. She has spoken to business and professional audiences throughout the United States, Europe, Canada and Asia.

Joan lives with her husband, Cliff, in Tonto Verde, Arizona. In addition to her relationship with Cliff, much joy in her life comes from her children, Bryan and Shelley, and from her grandchildren, Alea and Ethan.

A Woman Can Do That!
Quick Order Form

Fax orders: (480) 471-1181 Send this form.

Telephone orders: Call (877) 824-3014 toll-free.
Have your credit card ready.

E-mail orders: orders@leaderdynamics.com

Postal Orders: Leader Dynamics
Joan Gustafson
P.O. Box 19507
Fountain Hills, AZ 85269, USA.
Telephone: (480) 471-1171

Please send me:

_____ copies of *A Woman Can Do That!* @ $14.95

Total for books   _____

Arizona residents, add 7.2% sales tax   _____

Shipping: U.S. $4 for the first book   _____

$2 for each additional book   _____

International: $9 for the first book   _____

$5 for each additional book   _____

Total for Order: _____

Name:_____

Address: _____

City: _____ State:_____ Zip:_____

Country (if other than USA):_____

Telephone: _____ E-mail address:_____

Payment: ❑ Check or Money Order
Credit card:
❑ Visa   ❑ MasterCard   ❑ American Express   ❑ Discover

Card number:_____ Exp. date: _____

Signature:_____

Please also send information on the following:

❑ Related Seminars   ❑ Organizational Consulting

❑ Keynotes by Joan Gustafson   ❑ Personal/Professional Coaching